# VE DAY

## THE ALBUM

*Photographs from the*
*IMPERIAL WAR MUSEUM*

# JOHN DELANEY

Ebury Press
London

This edition published for Limited Editions in 1995
First published in 1995

1 3 5 7 9 10 8 6 4 2

Text copyright © John Delaney 1995
Photographs copyright © the Imperial War Museum

The right of John Delaney to be identified as the author
of this work has been asserted by him in accordance with the
Copyright, Designs and Patents Act 1988.

First published in the United Kingdom in 1995 by Ebury Press
Random House, 20 Vauxhall Bridge Road, London SW1V 2SA

Random House Australia (Pty) Limited
20 Alfred Street, Milsons Point, Sydney
New South Wales 2061, Australia

Random House New Zealand Limited
18 Poland Road, Glenfield
Auckland 10, New Zealand

Random House South Africa (Pty) Limited
PO Box 3317, Bergvlei, South Africa

Random House UK Limited Reg. No. 954009
British Library Cataloguing in Publication Data. A catalogue
record for this book is available from the British Library.

Edited by Mary Remnant and Malcolm Ward
Designed by Behram Kapadia

ISBN 0 09 180455 8

Printed and bound in Great Britain by Butler and Tanner Ltd
Frome, Somerset

Papers used by Ebury Press are natural recyclable products made
from wood grown in sustainable forests.

# CONTENTS

# INTRODUCTION

Fifty years have passed since the end of the Second World War in Europe. Fifty years have passed since the Nazi death camps were liberated, and the full horrors of fascism were revealed to the world. For all who worked and fought for the Allied victory of 8 May 1945 – VE Day – and for all who have lived in freedom since that date, it is a time for celebration and remembrance.

Millions of servicemen and civilians, from every corner of the globe, lost their lives to make that victory possible, and millions more endured suffering and hardship in the struggle. All of us owe our freedom to their courage and self-sacrifice, and it is to this above all that we should now pay tribute.

Two generations of children, myself included, have now grown to adulthood since the end of the war knowing little or nothing of the tremendous events which shaped the lives of their parents and grandparents. As fighting breaks out again in the Balkans and Russia, as the war in Bosnia demonstrates the ever-present dangers of a return to the ideology of 'ethnic cleansing', and as neo-fascists continue to terrorise Europe's minorities, we are reminded what the Allied victory fifty years ago still means. This is what *has* happened, this is what *can still* happen if we are not vigilant and if we do not remember.

In this book I have placed most emphasis on the final months and concluding campaigns of the war, when European peace was won at the cost of thousands of Allied servicemen's lives. That is the historic significance of VE Day. Yet we should not forget those servicemen who spent 1944 and 1945 fighting in the Far East against the forces of Germany's ally Japan. Their heroism, although outside the scope of the book, equalled that of the men and women who fought against the Nazi tyranny in Europe.

Many studies of the latter stages of the European war concentrate almost exclusively on the Allied drive through France and the Low Countries; vital though that was, I have also tried to do full justice to the campaigns in Italy and on the Eastern Front and their role in the defeat of Hitler.

The British people played a central part in the victory, but many other nations did so too. I have tried to acknowledge this by including many photographs describing their actions. For example, many British readers will be unaware of the presence of Brazilian soldiers in the front line in Italy, or of the massive casualties caused by Hitler's V1 flying bombs and V2 rockets on the citizens of Antwerp.

*VE Day – The Album* does not set out to be an all-encompassing history of the last months of the European war, but rather a pictorial chronicle of events. There is a chapter on each of the last ten months. I chose to begin in August 1944 because it was at this point that the inevitability of German defeat became apparent. In the months that followed the Allies advanced slowly but inexorably on all fronts. This advance cost many lives, but the end was in sight. I describe not only the actions of land forces involved in these final battles but also the vital contributions of the Allied navies and air forces.

The album contains over 200 photographs – many of them never before published – of the personalities and events that shaped this crucial period in our history, including the major battles, life on the home front, women at war, and the daily life of the front-line soldier.

I hope this book will serve as an accessible and informative account of the last months of the war against Germany, as a tribute to those who fought and died, and as a timely reminder of the lessons of history.

*John Delaney*

# AUGUST 1944

## *Breakout from Normandy*

**W**ESTERN FRONT. France. This month saw the Allied breakout from the Normandy beachhead and the ending of any hopes the Germans may still have harboured of defeating the invasion of France.

Aug 1. Preliminary operations such as 'Goodwood' and 'Cobra' had drawn in the German reserves and opened a gap in the enemy line through which US troops poured, heading initially for the Brittany peninsula and the important port of Brest. But it soon became apparent that in reality the breakthrough presented a great opportunity to encircle the German defence line.

2. This prospect became even more enticing when Hitler ordered eight Panzer divisions into the projected pocket to counter-attack the US breakthrough in the hope of restoring the situation.

6. The German attack began but due to the intense pressure being exerted on their line by British forces, only the 47th Panzer Corps could be spared for it. Allied air power played a decisive role in the defeat of the 'Mortain Counter-attack'. The offensive stalled almost immediately and two days later was back on its start line.

7. Montgomery ordered the commencement of 'Operation Totalize', a thrust south from Caen to begin on the evening of the 7th. This attack was to link up with the US 15th Corps sweeping around the southern flank of the Germans and enveloping them. The aim of these two operations was the destruction of two enemy armies and the collapse of the entire Western Front defences.

The Germans soon realized that potential disaster lay ahead and used the remnants of their armoured formations to hold open the neck of the pocket, near the town of Falaise. Nevertheless well over 50,000 German prisoners were taken and much equipment was captured or destroyed.

Although the German armies in Normandy were not totally destroyed, they were forced to retreat in disarray, and the speed and extent of the Allied advance put paid to any hopes they may have had of constructing a second line of defence along the Seine. From then on, although in places German units turned and fought, the advance through France was largely devoid of serious combat.

15. While the breakout from Normandy was taking place, the Allies launched 'Operation Dragoon', the invasion of southern France.

The British government had expressed doubts about the necessity for this assault, and wanted the men and resources allocated to a campaign in Italy and the Balkans. Suspicious of Soviet motives, they wanted to liberate as much of eastern Europe as possible before the Russian troops arrived. The Americans disagreed and the Free French lobbied hard for the invasion. The landings met with little opposition and soon after troops were pushing up the Rhône Valley towards central France.

The uprising to liberate Paris had begun on the 19th. The Resistance and Gendarmerie gaining much initial success. However, within two days the conflict had lapsed into stalemate. A cease-fire was arranged between the German garrison and the freedom fighters but it did not hold for long, the SS were too contemptuous of their 'civilian' opposition.

After the fighting resumed it became clear that without outside intervention many thousands of innocent civilians would die and large sections of the historic city would be destroyed. As a result, the 4th US Division and 2nd French Armoured Division were ordered to go to the aid of the Resistance. The first Allied units entered the city on the 25th.

20. The Americans had by now obtained bridgeheads over the Seine both north and south of Paris.

MEDITERRANEAN. Italy. The advance up the Italian peninsula, always a slow one, had been reduced to a crawl by the withdrawal of large numbers of troops for 'Operation Dragoon'. The city of Florence had been liberated on the 5th but the rest of the month saw little in the way of miles gained, the German defence being helped considerably by the mountainous terrain. By the middle of the month the British had reached the Gothic Line, a system of concrete bunkers and defences stretching across the entire width of Italy. A major offensive to crack this system of fortifications began on the 30th.

EASTERN FRONT. Meanwhile, early in the month, Kovno was captured by Russian forces, effectively isolating the Baltic states from Germany itself.

18. Soviet troops reached the border of East Prussia itself.

19. A counter-attack reopened a route between the countries, a rare success for the Germans.

22. Hitler's joy was short-lived however, for Rumania withdrew from the Axis and Finland, another German ally, signalled its intention to make peace with the Soviet Union.

30. The Ploesti oil-fields, the last remaining source of non-synthetic fuel for the Germans, fell to the Soviets. The next day they entered Bucharest.

Poland. Throughout August a battle had been raging in the capital, Warsaw. On the first of the month the Polish Home Army, the underground loyal to the government in exile, had launched a full-scale uprising, hoping to liberate the city before the Russians arrived. The Soviet advance suddenly stalled at the suburb of Praga, on the other side of the Vistula. Stalin insisted that the halt was necessary to resupply his forward units in the face of stiffening opposition. Churchill accused the Russians of stopping

*The three generals who all claimed to be the architects of victory in Normandy. From left to right, General George S. Patton, General Omar N. Bradley and General, later Field Marshal Sir Bernard L. Montgomery. Patton claimed the rapid advance by his Third Army had been the decisive factor. Bradley argued that it was in fact his 'Operation Cobra' which had punched a significant hole in the German left flank, allowing the advance to take place. Montgomery asserted that victory was achieved only because of his overall strategic plan. Without his drawing the German armoured reserves onto the British front with operations such as 'Goodwood' (launched 18 July) the German forces would have been far too strong for any American offensive to succeed.*
*In fact, all three were justified in their claims. Without the generalship of each the breakout could not have taken place.*
*Arguments between the commanders were to continue throughout the campaign, souring Allied relations, to the detriment of the efficient prosecution of the war.*

*opposite Although the pursuit through France was at times rapid, German troops did occasionally conduct fierce rearguard actions. Here a British Bren gunner covers the advance of his colleagues on a street corner in Lisieux on 22 August. Meanwhile a villager makes her liberator welcome by pouring him a glass of home-made cider.*

**above** *Although thousands of Germans fled Paris at the approach of the Allies, many remained in strategic locations, determined to put up a stiff fight. The Resistance, who declared a public uprising on 19 August, laid siege to many of these key buildings, taking prisoner dozens of Germans after sharp and often quite bloody fire fights. The Paris Commandant, General Dietrich von Choltitz, quickly recognized that resistance was useless and surrendered after a two-hour siege of his Hotel Meurice HQ. At 3.30 p.m. on the 25th General Choltitz signed the capitulation document in the presence of General Le Clerc, commander of the 2nd French Armoured Division, whose troops had helped liberate the city.*

**below** *Members of the Resistance and the Gendarmerie attempt to keep a crowd from taking vengeance upon a suspected collaborator. With the liberation of the city came the opportunity to settle old scores and many men and women were summarily executed by the mob. The suspect here has already been attacked more than once and without the help of his erstwhile enemies would not have survived.*

deliberately to give the Germans enough time to wipe out the Home Army, eliminating political opposition to Stalin.

**SEA**. Significant activity in August was confined to the transportation and successful landing of the 86,575 men and 12,250 vehicles taking part in 'Operation Dragoon'. The Allied navies also continued bringing in much needed supplies to forces in northern France. The rapid advance by the Allied ground forces caused an immense strain on their lines of supply and stores, petrol particularly grew increasingly short as the month went on.

**AIR**. The RAF Strategic Air Offensive against Germany continued with major raids on Stuttgart, Stettin, Kiel, Königsberg, Hamburg and Bremen. Priority was given to attacks on oil facilities and V weapon sites.

In addition bombers provided direct battlefield support for Allied ground forces and successfully interdicted German road and rail communications, severely disrupting the movement of German troops and raw material.

**HOME FRONT**. The V1 flying bomb menace continued to cause many innocent deaths in and around London.

2. Churchill announced in the House of Commons that 4,735 civilians had so far been killed by Hitler's terror weapon. Forty more incidents during August were to add significantly to this figure.

*Life on the Home Front in August was not free of danger and tragedy. Here a pensioner had gone to the pub while his wife prepared Sunday dinner. On his return he found his home a pile of rubble, destroyed by a V1 flying bomb. The dog at his feet survived the blast by hiding in the 'Morrison' shelter when the alarm sounded. His wife was not so lucky, she died in the explosion. The local bobby administers the standard remedy of the time for shock, a mug of hot, sweet tea.*

*Winston Churchill commenced a morale-boosting tour of Italy on the 11th. Reports had filtered back that British troops were unhappy at the press attention being given to the armies in Normandy and the fact that so many units had been withdrawn from Italy for the forthcoming invasion of southern France. Here, after his arrival, Churchill is presented with a bouquet of oleanders from four-year-old Marta Fisher before his inspection of an American Divisional HQ.*

4. Counter measures were however beginning to take effect. The new British jet fighter, the Gloster Meteor, claimed its first kill when a Flying Officer Dean of 616 Squadron managed to deflect a V1, tipping it over by using the thermal currents from his wing. By the end of the month only one in ten of the V1s launched were finding their targets.

17. A flying bomb fell on Lavender Hill, killing fourteen people on a passing bus and fourteen more in nearby buildings. On the same day a flying bomb exploded in Morden where on almost the same spot another had landed eight hours earlier. Several rescue workers were killed trying to dig out survivors of the previous blast.

23. A V1 landed on East Barnet killing 211 civilians working in a factory producing tank and fighter plane radios.

*A Sherman tank of the 1st French Armoured Division splashes ashore from its landing ship on 15 August, during the opening hours of 'Operation Dragoon', the Allied invasion of the south of France. The initial landings met with little German resistance and the Allied forces were able to push inland at a rapid pace.*

**above** *Eight hundred Germans march to their temporary prisoner-of-war pen near Falaise under the watchful eyes of American Military Police. Well over 50,000 Germans were captured in the Falaise pocket, but many thousands more managed to escape, including most of their high-ranking officers, when the Allies failed to fully close the trap. This stirred up more bad feeling between the Allied generals, Patton blaming his superiors for ordering him to stop short of total encirclement. Had the Allies been able to close the pocket before 16 August, nine of the eleven German armoured divisions in the west would have been trapped and perhaps a decisive blow to close the war could have been struck.*

**below** *A German assault gun lies blazing in a village street on the road to Falaise. A wounded Canadian infantryman receives attention from a medic. On 7 August the 51st Highland Division and the 2nd Canadian Division launched 'Operation Totalize' in an attempt to reach Falaise from Caen. Troops of Patton's US Third Army were to complete the encirclement. Due to stiff German resistance and lacklustre planning the gap was not fully sealed until the 21st, over 30,000 German troops managing to escape. The congested lanes of German troops struggling to retreat through the neck of the pocket provided plenty of targets for Allied aircraft circling above. About 10,000 Germans were killed in the retreat.*

**above** *Bing Crosby teams up with US film star Broderick Crawford and Corporals Doug Marshall and Colin Frampton to introduce 'Mark up the map', the BBC's Allied Expeditionary Force programme on 28 August. Its aim was to give up-to-date information on the progress of the Allied war effort on all fronts. Bing was speaking on the programme to introduce himself to the men at the front, where he would shortly be touring.*

**below** *George Formby was famed for his constant morale-boosting trips to visit the 'boys at the front'. During the war, George and his wife Beryl (far left) toured all theatres of operations, from North Africa to Burma, spending long periods of time with the troops. Here George entertains men of the Royal Engineers near the front line in Normandy.*

Soviet soldiers entered Bucharest on the 31st. Here a Gaz jeep full of Russians chat to Rumanian soldiers (far right and rear of jeep) who until the 23rd had been allies of Germany. Since the 25th, however, following a coup d'état, the Rumanians had been fighting with Soviet forces to rid their country of its German occupiers.

**below** The Women's Royal Naval Service (WRNS) performed a number of vital tasks during the war. Here three WRNS river pilots study their charts before sailing out to guide in Royal Naval vessels. All three, left to right, Pat McGuiness, Pat Turner and Pat Downing, known as the 'three Pats', were highly qualified, Pat Turner even being given the title 'Chief Pilot' for Plymouth, where the women were based.

An American corporal realizes that the hard slog from Normandy may have its rewards after all! A Parisienne wearing a Stars and Stripes blouse and a Free French Cross of Lorraine, welcomes her liberator.

Throughout the summer of 1944 the RAF continued its Strategic Air Offensive against Germany, with oil processing and storage facilities being priority targets. The attack on the synthetic oil refinery near Homberg on 27 August marked a return to daylight raids for the first time since 1941. Here a Lancaster from 619 Squadron returns home from a daylight sortie.

A British six pounder anti-tank gun on the edge of Caumont, Normandy.
By the beginning of August British and Canadian troops were preparing to
push south from Caen to Falaise to complement the American breakout.
Vital to this operation was the securing of an area for the start line of the
attack. Anti-tank guns provided a secure screen from German
reconnaissance forces trying to determine Allied intentions. Here a gun
crew covers a secondary road south to the German lines. An enemy half-
track knocked out the previous day can be seen in the background.

**left** When Florence fell on the 5th, special squads of British troops were given specific objectives to secure as soon as possible. One of these was the Villa Spelman, which had been used as the local Gestapo HQ. A platoon of No. 30 Commando assaulted the building in the hope of capturing secret documents and/or staff. Here Captain Shaw, the patrol leader and one of his men kick down the locked door at the entrance to the Villa.

**opposite above** Paris, 26 August. General de Gaulle leads a triumphant march down the Champs d'Elysees from the Arc de Triomphe to Notre Dame for a thanksgiving service on the city's liberation. The procession was brought under fire several times causing over 300 casualties but the General and his citizens pressed on and the service went ahead as planned.

**opposite below** Parisians huddle together as sniper fire interrupts their liberation celebrations on the 25th. Not all the German garrison had retreated and there were plenty of the Milice, the pro-German fascist militia left to cause considerable casualties amongst the populace and the Resistance who were struggling to free their capital.

**below** A Sherman tank of the 22nd Regiment, 6th South African Armoured Division enters Florence via the ancient Porta Romano gate. The Germans did not put up a fight for the southern half of the city, preferring to withdraw over the River Arno and hold the northern bank. The retreating Germans destroyed all the bridges in the city except the world-famous Ponte Vecchio.

# SEPTEMBER 1944

# *Belgium Freed, Dutch Stalemate*

**W**ESTERN FRONT. Belgium. Sept 1. British units neared the border. The advance through northern France had been much easier than expected and it was hoped that the liberation of the Low Countries would be the same. These hopes were to be shattered in the hard fighting of the month ahead.

3. The Guards Armoured Division liberated Brussels. Most of the German garrison wisely quit the capital before the British arrived, but a few, along with several Belgian traitors, were captured by the Resistance. The Germans were handed over to the British authorities and the collaborators executed after a 'fair trial'.

4. The 11th Armoured Division entered Antwerp. Crowds of joyful civilians came out on to the streets to welcome their liberators. But the Germans were not going to give up this city without a fight. Bullets, shells and grenades burst amongst the crowds causing many casualties.

Antwerp was a vital seaport for the Allies. Their lines of supply were becoming very stretched, and the capture of the city was necessary to enable stores to be brought in much nearer the front. Only this way could the pace of the Allied advance be maintained.

7. The battle for Antwerp was finally won. British forces were not able to establish a bridgehead over the River Scheldt and as a consequence were in a poor position to drive north from the city to cut off German forces in the Beveland peninsula. This was to become of vital importance, as this strip of land dominated the sea approaches to the port of Antwerp. Even though the British held the city no supplies could be unloaded. This oversight was to cost the Allies dear later in the campaign.

Holland. 9. The Allies entered Dutch territory for the first time when US forces drove into Maastricht.

The supply problems of the Allies were already beginning to make themselves felt further south in Lorraine, the area of operations for Patton's US Third Army. His tanks ground to a halt through lack of fuel. The same thing happened to the US First Army which was forced to stop just short of the German city of Aachen. All that could be managed were fighting patrols across the German border to assess the enemy troop strength in the Siegfried Line.

It was becoming clear that a co-ordinated plan was needed to reinvigorate the slowing Allied advance.

General Dwight D. Eisenhower was in favour of a broad front strategy with priority being given to the clearance of the Scheldt estuary. Patton felt that an attack in the south would break the deadlock and lead to a German collapse. Montgomery argued for a 'single full-blooded thrust' in his northern sector. Both Patton's and Montgomery's plans meant that supplies would have to be withheld from their opposite number, thus heightening their already intense rivalry.

Montgomery got his way. The direct result of his strategy was 'Operation Market-Garden', launched on the 17th.

This bold and imaginative plan aimed to catapult British troops into Germany along a narrow corridor of land through Holland. The Allied 1st Airborne Army was to be used to seize a series of key bridges ('Operation Market'), and then land forces were to pour over this airborne carpet into Germany ('Operation Garden').

17. A Sunday. The airborne armada set out from England, 1,068 aircraft carrying paratroopers (478 towing gliders were used to carry the 1st British Airborne Division alone).

The 101st US Airborne Division was to capture Eindhoven and the canal bridges to the north of the town. The 82nd US Airborne Division was to capture Nijmegen and two big bridges over the Meuse and the Waal. The British 1st Airborne Division was to capture the last bridge

**right** *A Soviet rifleman on the 1st Baltic Front covers three of his comrades as they cross a stream somewhere in Latvia.*
**opposite** *Two girls, one with an appropriated British officer's hat, ride on a Guards Armoured Division jeep through a throng of well-wishers welcoming the British to Brussels.*
**below** *Germans who were too slow to escape from the capital found themselves rounded up by the Belgian Resistance and placed on public view in Brussels zoo. Here a group of despondent-looking Germans sit in the lion's cage.*

# SEPTEMBER 1944

over the Lower Rhine, at Arnhem. At the same time the British 30th Corps, led by the Guards Armoured Division, attacked north from Belgium.

On the first day of operations the US 101st Airborne occupied Eindhoven and took the bridges over the Wilhelmina and Zuiter Willemsvaart canals. The 82nd captured the bridge over the Meuse at Grave but not that over the Waal at Nijmegen. The British 1st Airborne found the road to Arnhem blocked by powerful German forces. Only one battalion, the 2nd, managed to reach the bridge and it was soon cut off.

18. 30th Corps managed to link up with the US 101st Airborne north of Eindhoven. Both the 82nd US Airborne and the British 1st Airborne were still trying to break through to their objectives.

19. 30th Corps managed to link up with elements of the US 82nd Airborne at Grave. The bridge at Nijmegen was still in German hands. The British at Arnhem could not break through to relieve the exhausted paratroopers of the 2nd Parachute Battalion who were still hanging on to one end of the bridge. The British force had run into two SS Panzer divisions, recently sent to the area to rest and refit.

21. The bridge at Nijmegen was finally captured by a daring daylight river crossing by men of the US 82nd Airborne supported by tanks and men of the Grenadier Guards. The operation was now seventy-two hours behind schedule. The battalion at Arnhem bridge was finally forced to surrender after three days of continuous combat against vastly superior enemy forces. The rest of the 1st British Airborne Division now took up a defensive perimeter around the town of Oosterbeek to the west of Arnhem.

Over the next two days it became clear that the relief force would not arrive in time to save the 1st Airborne Division. The Guards Armoured Division were held up by stiff German resistance and slowed down by their own over-cautiousness. Many American and British paratroopers were to later lay the blame for the operation's failure on the 30th Corps's inordinately slow progress.

22. A brigade of Polish paratroopers were dropped to the south of the British bridgehead in the hope that they could form a link between the British paratroopers and the 30th Corps struggling to reach them. The air drop met with disaster, many of the Poles being killed as they

**above** *Men of the Royal Warwickshire Regiment, 8 Corps, wait to go forward against the enemy on the back of a Sherman tank in Holland on the 24th.*
**left** *On The 15th, at the Quebec Conference, President Roosevelt and Prime Minister Churchill agreed that the Morgenthau Plan for the deindustrialization of Germany would be implemented as soon as the war in Europe ended. The plan, which envisaged an agrarian and demilitarized society, was almost immediately vetoed by the US State Department. Joseph Goebbels, the German Minister of Propaganda, used the disclosed details of the plan to persuade the German population to fight on. Here the premiers involved in the talks pose for the photographers: clockwise Prime Minister Winston Churchill, the Earl of Athlone (Governor General of Canada), President Franklin D. Roosevelt and W.L MacKenzie King, Canadian Prime Minister.*

22

*American soldiers advance cautiously along a ruined street on the outskirts of Brest. The strategically important port was defended tenaciously by the Germans. It fell on the 19th, after a twenty-seven day siege, 35,000 prisoners being taken. A significant part of Patton's Third Army was tied up on the Brittany peninsula when they may have proved more effective adding weight to the US thrust through France.*

descended into the heart of the German positions. Only a very few managed to make it across the river to the trapped forces of the 1st Airborne.

25. Montgomery gave the order to evacuate the British troops back across the Lower Rhine. Only about 2,200 of the division's original 10,000 men made it to Allied lines.

The operation could well have been successful if carried out with more gusto by the 30th Corps and if the paratroopers had descended nearer to their objectives. The plan, although bold in concept, was too much of a gamble for Montgomery, a normally cautious general. His caution infected the officers below him, and the operation failed because of their lack of a sense of urgency.

France. 29. Canadian troops pushing towards Calais captured the great batteries on the Cap Gris Nez. These guns had been shelling the towns on the Kent coast since 1940. Nearly 3,000 shells fell on Dover alone and over 500 civilians were killed or wounded in the bombardments. The next day the remaining 7,000 men of the German garrison in Calais surrendered.

**MEDITERRANEAN.** Italy. Throughout the first week of September the British 8th Army continued its attack on the Gothic Line, defended tenaciously by the German 51st Mountain Corps and 76th Armoured Corps.

7. The Germans were forced to withdraw from their positions in the hills north and north-east of Florence.

13. The 8th Army took the Coriano and Gemmano Hills, an important section of the Gothic Line. The fighting for this series of fortifications continued, with San Marino falling on the 20th and Rimini liberated the next day. The Gothic Line was then irreparably broken. The 8th Army had lost 14,000 men killed, wounded and missing in

*Four Land Army girls smile happily as they bring in the last of the year's harvest. The WLA (Women's Land Army) performed a vital role in the Second World War, taking over the farm duties previously held by the men sent to the front. Without this organization food production would have suffered tremendously and Britain would have had an even harder time feeding herself during the lean war years.*

*Women's Land Army girls relax after a hard day's work on the farm by being taken for a coach ride by three US servicemen. They were used to more modern modes of transport being members of USAAF Transport Command, i.e. Dakota pilots ferrying supplies to the Allied Armies in Europe.*

breaking through the German defence line. Although forced back, the German 10th and 14th Armies continued to keep the Allied forces' advance down to a snail's pace.

**EASTERN FRONT.** Baltic. 16. A major Russian offensive began.

22. The Estonian capital Tallinn was captured. The German forces in the area were now cut off from East Prussia. However, they skilfully retreated into the Courland Peninsula where an evacuation by sea to Germany was begun.

Poland. Throughout September the uprising in the Polish capital continued, with the patriots losing more and more of the city to the Germans. Finally, on the 18th, Stalin allowed US planes to refuel at Soviet airfields, 107 American bombers flying on a mission to drop supplies to the beleaguered defenders. The Russians also dropped a token amount of arms and ammunition. Most fell straight into German hands, as they now controlled the majority of the city. The Russian supplies collected by the remnants of the Home Army were found to be mostly inoperative due to the failure of the aircrews to attach parachutes to the supply canisters. The slow elimination of the Polish patriots was the only tangible success of the month on the Eastern Front for the Germans.

Balkans. At the end of the first week of September Soviet forces were close to the borders of both Bulgaria and Yugoslavia. The Germans began a full-scale retreat from Greece recognizing that they could be cut off if the Soviets reached the Aegean.

The Russians were aided in Yugoslavia by Tito's Partisans and in Bulgaria the government ordered its forces not to resist the advancing Red Army. By the 8th Bulgaria was no longer a member of the Axis but was fighting alongside the Russians against Germany.

**AIR.** Throughout September the RAF and USAAF continued with their Strategic Air Offensive against Germany. Initially synthetic oil production plants were the prime targets but with the appearance of the new Me262 jet fighter the emphasis was once again switched to aircraft production facilities.

During this period Bomber Command launched ten attacks in support of ground forces, mainly against German fortified positions, including bombardments of the Channel port of Calais. Thirty-five area bombing raids on German cities were also carried out. In one attack, on the night of 11/12 September, over 10,000 people, mainly civilians, were killed.

On the 15th the RAF attempted to sink the German battleship *Tirpitz* at anchor in the Kaa Fjord in Norway. Although the attack did not manage to sink the ship, the damage inflicted on her was so great that she was considered impracticable to repair and was towed south to be used as a static gunship.

The RAF and USAAF also provided several thousand aircraft for 'Operation Market-Garden'. Transport aircraft,

**above** *A Bren gun team of the 3rd Canadian Infantry Division in the ruins of Boulogne on the 21st. The seaport finally fell the next day, after the town had been reduced to rubble by intense fighting. Hitler had decreed that all major channel ports be held until the last man to deny the Allies the means to effectively supply their troops in the field in France.*
**right** *One of the few photographs ever taken of actual defenders of the bridge at Arnhem. These three men, left to right, Sapper J. Dinney, Sapper C. Grier and Lance Corporal R. Robb, were members of the 1st Parachute Squadron, Royal Engineers, who, along with the 2nd Battalion the Parachute Regiment, held the bridge for three days. This task had been allotted to the whole 1st Airborne Division, who were told they would have to hold out for only forty-eight hours. This photograph was taken shortly after their capture, at approximately 3.30 p.m. on the 20th, after their defensive position, the Van Limburgstirum School, just east of the bridge, had been overrun by the enemy. They had been fighting continuously for over sixty hours and look close to complete exhaustion.*

bombers and fighter escorts were all used in large numbers to support the ill-fated attack into Holland.

HOME FRONT. 6. The blackout in towns and cities across the country was eased. The Luftwaffe very rarely ventured into British air space and the blackout in no way countered the V1 flying bombs. These continued to fall throughout the month but in significantly less numbers now that most of their launching sites had been captured by the Allied advance.

5. The Germans did try launching V1s from Heinkel bombers over the North Sea but their loss rate was

prohibitive; of sixty-six bombers carrying flying bombs on this day, forty either crashed or were shot down. The practice was soon discontinued.

8. A new type of weapon fell on Britain for the first time, the V2 rocket. The explosion in Staveley Road, Chiswick, killed three people. The V2 was potentially a far more dangerous weapon than the V1. Its approach was undetectable and there was therefore no way of intercepting it.

**left** *Vincento Biscardo, a fourteen-year-old Italian boy whose family had been killed in the fighting, was adopted by the 34th US Division HQ Military Police, then stationed in Florence. 'Sergeant' Biscardo, as well as becoming the unofficial HQ mascot, was trained by the police and undertook duties in the city. Here he takes time out from directing traffic to talk to his friend, nine-year-old Elena Cimballi.*
**opposite** *Sub-Lieutenant K.C.J. Robinson at the hydroplane controls of midget submarine X-24. This X-Craft, as they were known, took part in a daring raid against a giant floating dock in Bergen, Norway on the 14th. The craft had to carefully navigate thirty miles of off-shore islands, a minefield and anti-submarine booms before being able to destroy the German facility. The submarine, captained by Lieutenant H.P. Westmacott on his second foray into Bergen's coastal waters, managed to return safely to base.*
**below** *The last moments of an American consolidated B-24 Liberator after an attack by German fighters over Austria. This plane was one of a squadron flying from Italy to bomb the river traffic on the Danube, a vital supply route for the Third Reich. Between April and September supplies moved by river had been reduced by almost 70 per cent.*

**below** *A Dakota full of paratroopers of the 1st British Airborne Division en route for Holland on the 17th. One of the main reasons for the failure of the operation was that the drop zones were eight miles to the west of the objective, the bridge over the Lower Rhine at Arnhem. The RAF were worried that to drop nearer the bridge would cause many unnecessary casualties from anti-aircraft fire. As it was, the failure to capture the objective quickly gave the Germans time to react and block the route to the bridge, only 700 or so British paratroopers slipping through the German lines.*

**left** A lieutenant of the US 82nd Airborne Division explains the platoon objective to his rather sceptical-looking men before they embark on the 17th. Two US Airborne Divisions, the 82nd and 101st took part in 'Operation Market-Garden'. The 82nd was to capture the bridges at Grave and Nijmegen, the 101st was to secure Eindhoven and the bridges over the canals to the north of the town. By holding these crossings, the US troops along with the 1st British Airborne Division were to form a carpet over which the armoured forces of 30 Corps would pass into Germany, hopefully to end the war in 1944. Both US divisions managed to achieve their objectives, although Nijmegen was captured far behind schedule and only after a daring daylight river crossing by men of the US 82nd Airborne Division.

**below** Hundreds of British parachutes descend on to the fields near Wolfheze on the 17th. The 1st Parachute Brigade and 1st Air Landing Brigade faced almost immediate opposition from an SS training battalion who happened to be on exercise in the area. The delay caused to the advance on the bridge at Arnhem allowed elements of the 9th SS Panzer Division 'Hohenstaufen' to place themselves across the intended path of the British forces. The battle at Arnhem almost immediately became one of the British attempting to batter their way through to the bridge rather than digging in to defend it.

On the 10th Le Havre, one of Hitler's channel port bastions, fell to a concerted attack by the British 49th and 51st Divisions. Armour of all types was used, including flail and flame-thrower tanks. Here a Squadron of Churchill infantry tanks waits to go into action on the outskirts of the port.

The men of the 1st British Airborne Division grimly held on, hoping in vain that 30 Corps would arrive to relieve them. By the 23rd many ad hoc units of British paratroopers, artillerymen and glider pilots held the perimeter. Here just such a group advance through the ruins of a house in Oosterbeek.

# OCTOBER 1944

# *A Long Hard Slog to the Reich*

WESTERN FRONT. October saw the end of any hopes the Allies may have had of winning the war quickly. A Cabinet meeting in London on the 2nd, attended by Eisenhower and Montgomery, decided that Germany could not be defeated until the spring of 1945. Enemy defences had stiffened considerably in the last month, and the Siegfried Line covering the German frontier looked to be a difficult obstacle to overcome. October would be spent probing these fortified defences, looking for weaknesses and clearing up the remaining pockets of resistance remaining in France and the Low Countries. Northern Holland could no longer look forward to imminent liberation. Allied eyes now turned east to Germany itself. Eisenhower's plan of a broad front advance was adopted. It was therefore important that no enemy forces be left east of the Rhine. A secure base was needed to form the jump-off point for an assault into the Reich.

Germany. Oct 3. US forces staged their first large-scale assault into the country, crossing the River Wurm and gaining a small foothold in the Siegfried Line.

4. A German armoured counter-attack attempted to drive the US troops back but with little success. The Americans pressed on towards their objective, the first major city of the Third Reich, Aachen.

8. US forces surrounded the city in a pincer movement.

13. The assault on Aachen began. There followed a week of intense fighting, the US 1st Infantry Division having to clear the city street by street.

21. Aachen captured. A key position in the Siegfried Line, its fall was a significant achievement for the Allied cause.

Fighting continued to the end of the month all along the Allied line, clearing pockets of resistance and preparing the way for a thrust across the Rhine into the heart of Germany.

France. Throughout the first week of the month fighting continued in northern France with a bitter battle for the port of Dunkirk.

Holland. The US 7th Armoured Division and British 11th Armoured Division made slow progress in their advance to Overloon and Venray. Their objective was to clear enemy troops from the east bank of the Maas to enable an assault into Germany from Holland to take place.

16. Overloon fell but British units, including the 11th Armoured Division, 3rd Infantry Division and 6th Guards Tank Brigade found it a very tough task to throw back the German defenders.

27. Tilburg and Bergen op Zoom were liberated.

Belgium. 9. Canadian forces landed at Breskens on the

**above** *A Soviet T34 tank roars down a street in Belgrade on the 20th, cheered on by the city's liberated citizenry.*
**opposite** *A Soviet Guards infantry unit attacks a wooded German position south-east of Riga, Latvia, covered by the fire of a machine-gun team and supporting infantry.*

south side of the Scheldt estuary. Their aim was to trap General Gustav Adolf von Zangen's 15th Army which was attempting to cross the river to Beveland and Walcheren. The fighting was particularly unpleasant in this sector. Large areas of land had been flooded and men often found themselves in combat waist-deep in icy water. The south bank of the estuary was cleared of the enemy, but the use of Antwerp was still denied to the Allies, German troops on Walcheren and Beveland still dominating the approaches to the port. A sea-borne landing to open the city to Allied shipping was planned for early November.

MEDITERRANEAN. Italy. The Brazilian Expeditionary Force was sent into the front line as part of the US Fifth Army's drive on Bologna. General Mark W. Clark's attempts to reach the city cost the Allies dearly, over 550 men being killed or wounded on each day of the offensive. Further to the east the British 8th Army also had little luck against strong German opposition. The autumn rains came early to Italy, slowing down the Allied advance even more. The River Marecchia rose over six feet. A few days ago men had easily waded across.

27. The Allied offensive ground to a halt. The rains and the early onset of winter put paid to any further major offensives that year.

Greece. British Commandos and Greek troops began to liberate the Greek islands still under Nazi control.

2. The British landed at Lemnos, Levita and Mtilini. The next day they set foot on Crete in force, for the first time since their evacuation in 1941.

4. British paratroopers landed on the Greek mainland, followed a day later by seaborne troops. The Germans were everywhere retreating, determined to evacuate the country before being cut off by the advancing Red Army. The campaign in Greece became a pursuit of rapidly retreating Germans. They stood and fought only in very few places.

10. Corinth liberated.

14. The first British troops enter Athens alongside Greek Partisans, the Germans abandoning the capital without a fight. The main British occupation forces arrived over the next few days.

21. Belgrade, the Yugoslavian capital, is liberated by troops of Tito's Army of National Liberation, followed closely by Soviet units. The escape route north for German Army Group E looked more tenuous by the day.

EASTERN FRONT. Finland. 2. The Soviet Army crossed the border into northern Finland to pursue retreating German forces into Norway. Finnish troops carefully avoided any entanglement in the fighting.

**above** *Troops from the 1st Proletarian Division of Tito's Yugoslav Army of National Liberation enter Belgrade on the 20th. With only limited help from the Allies, this guerrilla army had evicted the occupying Germans from their homeland after three years of savage warfare.*

**below** *Soviet artillery passes through the ruined town of Eydtkuhnen, East Prussia, half-way between Kovno and Königsberg.*

The Germans stubbornly defended every street of Aachen, the first major city of the Third Reich to be attacked by the Allies. Here, on the 15th, a 57 mm anti-tank gun fires on a tower at the far end of a main street to clear it of snipers before the infantry advance.

Soft transport of the 4th British Infantry Division struggle to cross a flooded stream in Italy on the 26th. The autumn rains came earlier than expected and were the heaviest for many years. The Allied advance, already slowed by the mountainous terrain, came to an almost complete stop.

By the end of the month the rains had moved north and affected France and the Low Countries, bringing the advance down to a crawl in all sectors. It was going to be a long hard slog to the Reich. Here a US Army artillery unit fords a flooded main street in a town in Alsace-Lorraine.

25. Russian troops crossed the border into Norway to liberate the Arctic town of Kirkenes.

Baltic. 5. A major offensive towards the Latvian capital, Riga, began. The day after that Russian troops crossed the border into Czechoslovakia. Things looked increasingly grim for the Germans.

10. The Soviet forces reached the Baltic sea, cutting off the garrison in Riga from East Prussia.

15. The Latvian capital finally fell.

18. It is announced that all men between sixteen and sixty are to be called up for the Volkssturm (the German Home Guard). This will enable an increase in the size of the German armed forces but the fighting quality of untrained pensioners and schoolboys left a lot to be desired.

19. The Soviet advance pushed on into East Prussia. Four days later it was only forty-five miles from the 'Wolf's Lair', Hitler's HQ in Rastenburg.

Poland. 2. As the Red Army crossed into Finland, the surviving troops of the Polish Home Army surrendered to German forces in Warsaw. Over 15,000 had been killed in the fighting while the Germans suffered 10,000 dead. Tragically, some 200,000 Polish civilians became casualties during the battle which had razed most of the city to the ground.

Hungary. 9. One of the largest tank battles since Kursk raged on the Hungarian plains. Elements of German Army Group South managed to encircle three Soviet tank corps. Fighting alongside the Russians were their new allies, the Rumanians. Hungarian forces still assisted the Germans even though a secret delegation had been in Moscow since the first of the month discussing terms for surrender.

15. The Germans had their suspicions, and when the country's leader, Admiral Nikolaus Horthy, broadcast to the nation that he was willing to come to terms, he was immediately deposed in a coup led by SS Major Otto Skorzeny. The new government was headed by Ferenc Szalasi, leader of the Hungarian fascist movement, the Arrow Cross.

30. Budapest looked to be the next capital to fall. The Soviet 6th Guards Tank Army were smashing their way through the Hungarian 3rd Army, who were defending the main routes to the city.

Yugoslavia. 4. Soviet forces crossed the Danube, capturing the town of Pancevo.

AIR. On the 3rd the RAF began to prepare for the forthcoming invasion of Walcheren by bombing the dyke that kept the sea from engulfing large parts of the island. Lancasters dropped 12,000 lb 'Tallboy' bombs on the dyke near Westkapelle, opening up a 120-yard gap in the sea wall. The bombing made movement around the island impossible for the German garrison, helping the invaders to defeat the defenders in detail.

Lancasters of 617 Squadron also breached the Kembs Dam on the Upper Rhine. This time the objective was not to inhibit the movement of the enemy but to make sure that the Germans could not blow the dam at a later date to slow up the Allied advance.

Early in the month the RAF twice attacked the U-boat yards at Wilhelmshaven, once in daylight, once at night. Between the 13th and 15th the Ruhr was the target of concerted Allied air attack, Duisberg being bombed by

1,013 RAF Lancasters and Halifaxes and 1,251 USAAF Flying Fortresses and Liberators. On the 31st Cologne was the target with 493 bombers dropping 4,000 tons of bombs and incendiaries. On the same day 671 USAAF bombers attacked oil installations throughout the area.

As well as the Strategic Air Offensive aimed at crippling Germany's war industry and breaking her citizens' will to fight on, the RAF mounted many smaller but still important raids on enemy facilities. On the 25th, in a low level bombing raid, a squadron of Typhoons destroyed a German HQ in the Dutch city of Dordrecht. A conference of high-ranking Wehrmacht officers was being held in the building. Ninety-four were killed including two generals. On the last day of the month twenty-four RAF Mosquitoes carried out a precision attack on the University of Aarhus in Denmark, which was being used as a Gestapo HQ. The aim of the mission was to destroy files and documents which were to be used to track down members of the Danish underground. As a fortunate by-product the bombing released several Resistance members being held as prisoners in the building, and 150 Gestapo members and several Danish informers were killed in the attack.

A second attempt was made on the 29th to sink the *Tirpitz*. Thirty-six Lancasters attempted to sink the vessel at her moorings in Tromsö Fjord. This time, due to a very effective smokescreen laid by the German defenders, the bombing was ineffective, not one hitting the vessel.

As the V2 attacks increased, the RAF began a sustained bombing campaign against their launch sites. Beginning on the 15th, the 2nd Tactical Air Force carried out over 10,000 bomber sorties and 600 fighter sweeps before the end of the month. Nevertheless, during October sixty-three V2s landed in Britain.

London was not the only target for the rockets. Between 25 September and 5 October sixteen V2s dropped in and around Norwich. Nor were attacks confined to Britain. In an attempt to keep the port of Antwerp closed, Hitler ordered that V2s be fired against the city. Two landed on the 13th, one killing thirty-two civilians. V1 flying bombs were also used. On the same day one exploded in the municipal slaughterhouse and killed fourteen civilians, most of them butchers waiting for the weekly meat ration. Six days later forty-four civilians were killed when another V2 landed on the city.

Men of the US 1st Infantry Division load captured shells and high explosives on to a tram they have nicknamed 'the Aachen Express'. The tram was then rolled down the street into the German positions where it was detonated. The V-13 'Aachen Express', was the second tram to be used in this fashion against the defenders of the city.

**below** During October King George VI went on a morale-boosting tour of the Western Front. On the 14th he visited Eisenhower at the US First Army HQ. Here the US generals present pose with the king on the steps of the HQ building. Front row, His Majesty King George VI (left) General Eisenhower, Commander Allied Forces Europe (right) back row, General Bradley, Commander US 12th Army Group (left) and General Courtney Hodges, Commander US First Army.

**below** Winston Churchill and Joseph Stalin, although coming from opposite ends of the political spectrum, got on famously throughout the Moscow Conference, each man appreciating the other's grasp of Realpolitik. At a meeting on the 9th they rather arbitrarily divided up zones of influence in post-war Europe without thinking to consult the governments of the nations concerned. Their cordial personal relations did not however overcome each man's deep suspicion of the other's motives. Churchill was far more apprehensive of communist strategy than was Roosevelt, who felt that the differences between the Great Powers could be settled by negotiation. As events were to later show, Churchill had a far better grasp of Stalin's plans than did the US President.

*Marlene Dietrich often toured the front raising the morale of the troops. Here she entertains a group of American GIs. Accompanying her (far left) were Joey Faye and pianist Jerry Cummings.*

*A series of three photographs taken secretly by a US Signal Corps photographer showing the reaction of German civilians fleeing the fighting in Aachen to the Nazi regime. A swastika flag was spread on the ground to see if German civilians would respectfully walk around it or pick it up. The results of the experiment were astonishing. The first old lady to cross the flag simply walked straight over it as if it were not there. A little later another old woman passed over the flag. This time she paused to wipe her feet vigorously upon it. She then walked off. A few steps down the street she stopped, turned around, walked back to the flag and spat upon it. Goebbels's propaganda broadcasts had obviously had little effect on the morale of many of the Reich's citizens.*

Between the 26th and 28th, aircraft from HMS Mauritius took part in attacks on enemy shipping off the Norwegian coast in the Bodö area. Nineteen enemy ships and one U-boat were sunk or severely damaged. Here a flight of Barracudas head out to attack an enemy convoy.

**opposite** An RAF Handley Page Halifax bomber flies over its target, the synthetic oil plant at Wanne-Eickel in the Ruhr, on the 12th. The bombing offensive against Germany's oil industry began to pay dividends as the war went on. First the Luftwaffe and then the Wehrmacht were hamstrung through lack of fuel.

On the 29th the two Royal Princesses, Elizabeth and Margaret, visited HMS King George V before she left to join Britain's East Indies Fleet. Here Commander J. G. Long, captain of the battleship, explains the routine of ammunitioning to Princess Elizabeth.

**below** Women not only served in the forces on the Home Front but also helped the Allies keep up the pace of their advance on Continental Europe. Here a group of girl mechanics from the ATS (Auxiliary Territorial Service) repair army transport at a workshop in Brussels on the 31st.

Men of the 1st Company the Oxfordshire and Buckinghamshire Light Infantry take cover on the outskirts of Heike on the 23rd during heavy fighting for the town.

Millions of German children who had grown up during the 1930s knew nothing but Hitler's dictatorship. Nazi indoctrination had taught them to revere their Führer almost as a god. As Allied troops crossed the frontier into Germany, they occasionally came across fanatic children who were determined to die for their Führer. Here two boys, Willy Etschenberg, aged fourteen (left) and Hubert Heinrichs, aged ten (right) are escorted around a prison courtyard for their daily exercise. Both had been caught sniping at American troops. The two boys were members of their local Hitler Youth group.

**above** *Early in October US forces crossed the German border in force for the first time. By the 3rd the town of Übach had been captured. Here a Sherman tank of the US First Army drives down the main street past a line of captured Germans heading in the opposite direction.*

*It is a little-known fact that the Brazilians sent a substantial amount of troops to fight with the Allies. The BEF (Brazilian Expeditionary Force) consisted of an infantry division and associated support units fighting under US command in the Italian theatre. Here a group of pilots from a Brazilian fighter squadron, part of the US 12th Air Force, are briefed on their next mission.*

# OCTOBER 1944

German troops often left behind booby traps as they retreated slowly into the Reich. A favourite was to stretch piano wire at head height across shaded roads. Motorcyclists and drivers of open-topped jeeps would then be seriously injured, in many cases decapitated. As a safety measure metal bars were added to the front of many vehicles. Here two dispatch riders, Sergeant D. Wilson and Corporal W. Wright demonstrate how this DIY conversion would snap the wire before it reached the head of the rider.

**below** Men of the 51st Highland Division fight their way through Bokstal on the 25th. A group of Dutch civilians crouch in a trench taking cover from the fighting going on around their homes.

# NOVEMBER 1944

# *Tidying Up*

**W**ESTERN FRONT. The Allies launched several offensives this month, the objectives of which were to drive the Germans back to the Rhine and eliminate any pockets of resistance cut off by their advance.

Holland. Nov 1. The British launched a seaborne invasion of Walcheren island, along with an assault across the Scheldt estuary from Breskens to Flushing on the Beveland peninsula. The heavy air bombardment to soften the German defences was cancelled due to the bad weather. Troops of the German 70th Infantry Division defended the island. This unit had been given the nickname 'Weissen Brot', due to the special bread ration provided for the men, most of whom suffered with stomach complaints. Men of 41st Royal Marine Commando landed at Westkapelle on the western tip of the island while the Canadian 4th Brigade and elements of the 52nd Lowland Division crossed the Scheldt.

3. The Polish 1st Armoured Division, part of British 1st Corps, began yet another offensive against German troops in Holland on the south side of the river Maas. They were joined the next day by the 49th and 104th Divisions. The area had to be cleared of the enemy if an assault into Germany from the northern end of the Allied line could take place.

4. Resistance in Flushing collapsed.

6. Middelburg, the most important town on Walcheren, fell to the Canadian 2nd Corps.

8. The last German defenders of Walcheren surrendered. Over 8,000 prisoners were taken in the operation.

14. In the north, a further British offensive was opened to reduce the German bridgehead west of the Maas, between Venlo and Roermond.

By the 21st British troops of the 49th and 51st Divisions were nearing their objective of Venlo.

Belgium. On the 2nd units of the 7th Armoured Division opened an offensive to drive the enemy from the Canal du Nord, north of Antwerp. The next day German resistance finally ended in the Breskens pocket. Slowly the Allies were eliminating the troublesome enemy positions left behind during the rapid advance of August and early September.

Germany. Patton, Commander of the US Third Army, decided to launch his offensive through the Saar to the Rhine on the 8th, despite the dreadful weather conditions which were preventing any air activity.

Through mid-November 'Operation Queen', the offensive to clear German forces from the area north of Aachen continued, with elements of the US 29th Division reaching the outskirts of Jülich on the 18th. On the same

*Soviet troops prepare to bombard an enemy strongpoint with a mobile 155 mm howitzer, East Prussia.*

**opposite** *Russian infantry advance past a burning farmhouse, southeast of Klaipeda, Memel.*

day, further north, British forces launched 'Operation Clipper'. This was an attempt to capture the Geilenkirchen salient, another German-held area protruding behind the Allied lines.

Throughout the last week of November Allied troops continued to push back the enemy despite ever-worsening weather conditions. The Germans did however have some localized successes. In the offensive around Aachen in the Hürtgen forest sector US forces were stopped dead in their tracks, the 4th Division suffering particularly heavy losses.

France. The US 20th Corps opened the US Third Army offensive, pushing towards the French fortress city of Metz. The Moselle was crossed by the US 90th and 95th Infantry Divisions and south of the city the US 5th Infantry Division gained a bridgehead across the River Seille.

12. The Germans launched a counter-attack to try and throw the Americans back across the Moselle but were defeated with heavy losses. They did however succeed in destroying the bridge across the river at Cattenom.

14. The southern end of the Allied line, the French 1st Army, began its attack on Belfort, which it entered the next day. The fighting for the city was severe and lasted for several days.

19. By now, Metz had been completely surrounded.

23. Troops of the French 2nd Division entered the outskirts of Strasbourg.

25. The fortress city of Metz finally fell to the besieging Americans of the US Third Army.

MEDITERRANEAN. In the Italian theatre of operations events moved much more slowly for the Allies. Although there were advances during November, they were necessarily limited because of the mountainous terrain and the early onset of the Italian winter. The Polish 2nd Corps managed to take Monte Testa, Monte Chiodo and Monte Pratello, German positions previously overlooking the Allied line. The British 4th and 46th Divisions of 5th Corps managed to capture Forli on the 9th. Later in the month the 46th Division also liberated Castiglione. Progress was slow and little else of note was achieved during the month.

EASTERN FRONT. Norway. On the 22nd, Soviet forces in the far north resumed their offensive against the German 20th Mountain Army, this time with the active support of Finnish units which had recently linked up with the Red Army.

Baltic. The German Army Group North was still cut off in northern Latvia. Some supplies came in and a few evacuees left courtesy of the German Navy, which still had a strong presence in the area.

*In early November Norwegian troops who had escaped to Britain after their country's occupation in 1940 returned to fight alongside Soviet forces on the Petsamö front in northern Norway. Here infantrymen on the deck of HMS Berwick listen to a speech given by their commanding officer, Colonel Arne Dahl, as they near the disembarkation point.*

Hungary. The month began with the capture of Kecskemet to the south-east of Budapest. The Soviets pressed hard, as they believed the capital would soon be within their grasp.

4. The Soviet advance did not resume until the 18th when the Leningrad front attacked enemy forces holding on to Saaremaa island in the Gulf of Riga. The Russian offensive came to a standstill, stiffening German resistance, and a deterioration in the weather combined to stop the advance.

23. The rail centre of Csap was captured. This was a major blow to the Germans as it effectively disrupted most of their supply routes through the country. On the same day Russian troops reached the Danube to the south of Budapest.

27. Soviet troops of the 2nd Ukrainian Front captured Hatvan to the north-east of Budapest, beginning the encirclement of the city.

30. The Rumanian 4th Army captured Eger. The net around the capital was now almost closed.

BALKANS. The slow retreat of Army Group E up the Balkans continued, the Red Army still attempting to reach the Adriatic and cut off their withdrawal.

20. All German troops had been evacuated from Greece, except for outlying islands, where several thousand men were trapped. On the same day the Army Group was busily evacuating Albania, troops abandoning the capital, Tirana.

29. Army Group E abandoned Scutari in Albania.

30. They linked up with German units fighting against the Soviets in Hungary. The front was temporarily stabilized along a line from Mostar to Visegrad on the River Drina. This defence held until 13 January.

AIR. The pounding of Germany's cities and industry continued without let-up. During the day the USAAF regularly bombed targets in the Hamburg, Hanover and Saarbrucken areas. At night the RAF attacked the Ruhr with regular concentrations of over 1,000 bombers. On the 18th, 402 Lancasters attacked Berlin, the first of a series of sixteen air attacks on the German capital. The raid caused extensive damage and thousands of casualties. Only nine bombers were lost.

Bombing in direct support of ground operations also continued. The heaviest attack of its type took place on the 16th, 2,807 American and British bombers obliterating the towns of Jülich, Duren and Heinsberg before an attack by elements of the US 1st and 9th armies. Ground attack

*Between the 20th and 30th, Royal Navy mine-sweepers were brought in to clear the Scheldt estuary of mines and underwater obstacles left by the Germans. This was necessary to make the port safe for supply ships. Here the crew of Mine-sweeper 2189 (**right**) fire at a mine floating off the starboard side of their vessel. In the other photograph the mine can be seen exploding.*

missions were of great help to the Allied ground forces trying to capture Walcheren island, over 10,000 ground support sorties being flown by RAF rocket-carrying Typhoon aircraft in the first eight days of the operation.

On the 12th the RAF finally managed to sink the *Tirpitz*. The attack was carried out in Tromsö Fjord by thirty-two Lancasters carrying 12,000 lb 'Tallboy' bombs. The ship was hit three times, turning completely over at anchor. Of its 1,800 crew just over 800 were rescued.

Throughout November Hitler's V weapons continued to be targeted at London and other British cities within range of their launch sites in Northern Europe. Increasingly they were also launched at Continental cities such as Antwerp in an attempt to disrupt Allied supply lines. On the 27th, the day after the first convoy into the port, a V2 exploded near the railway station killing 157 people, 29 of them British servicemen who had arrived by ship the previous day. At the height of the attacks on the city a V1 or V2 landed every twelve and a half minutes. Nevertheless the Allies were still able to use the docks to bring in 25,000 tons of much needed supplies every day.

SEA. Throughout November the Royal Navy kept Allied supplies moving across the Channel. It also continued to convoy much-needed weapons, vehicles and raw material to Russia via the Arctic Ocean, an area still rife with U-boat and Luftwaffe bomber activity. In direct support of land operations they supplied gunfire support for the invasion of Walcheren, although the actual damage inflicted on the German defenders was slight.

The crews of the landing craft that delivered the infantry to the shore line showed a high degree of bravery in carrying through a very dangerous job. The crews referred to their LSTs (Landing Ship Tanks) as Large Slow Targets because of the ease with which the Germans could hit them with their shore guns. During the operation to land troops at Westkapelle, nine of the twenty-eight craft taking part were sunk and a further eleven damaged.

The Royal Navy also played a vital role in reopening Antwerp for the Allies, the first ship arriving in the Scheldt on the 4th. It took over two weeks of dangerous work by mine-sweepers and divers to clear the estuary and make it safe for shipping.

A Sherman crab flail tank disembarks from its landing craft during the invasion of Walcheren on the 2nd. The chains or flails when rotated beat a path in front of it, exploding any mines they hit.

**below** A Landing Craft (Support) sinks after being hit by shell fire during the invasion of Walcheren on the 1st. These vessels were equipped with guns to give close-range fire support to the landing craft carrying the infantry assault. This one had approached to within sixty yards of a German shore battery but had lost the duel with its emplaced guns.

HOME FRONT. On the 25th, in London, a V2 rocket hit the Woolworth's store in New Cross Road, Deptford, killing 160 lunchtime shoppers. It was the highest casualty rate from any single V weapon attack so far. During November another explosion, this time accidental, claimed a further 68 civilian lives. On the 27th, in Fauld, Staffordshire, a massive blast ripped apart an underground bomb store. Not only were workers in the mine killed but several farmers in the fields over ninety feet above also lost their lives.

**above** *On the 1st, along with the seaborne landing at Westkapelle, troops were ferried across the Scheldt from Breskens to Flushing. After three days of fighting the port was cleared of the enemy. Here on the 4th British troops advance through the outskirts of the town in pursuit of the retreating Germans. The landings on Walcheren island went very successfully and at last opened the port of Antwerp to Allied shipping.*

A group of British infantrymen, all wearing their life jackets, drink mugs of tea before embarking on to their landing craft for the attack on Walcheren on the 1st.

Buffalo and Weasel vehicles disembark from LCT (Landing Craft Tank) 532 on to a Walcheren beach on the 1st. The two lead vehicles, the Buffaloes, carry Royal Marine Commandos who are to attack the town of Westkapelle, which can be seen in the background.

*The invasion of Walcheren island on the 1st. A landing craft just about to disgorge its complement of Royal Marine Commandos and their amphibious Buffalo vehicles. The burning town of Westkapelle can be seen in the background.*

*British and Dutch Royal Marine Commandos prepare to move off across the Scheldt from Breskens to Flushing on the 3rd.*

*Rabbi Herman Dicker of Brooklyn, New York, serving with the US Third Army, returns the sacred scroll to the Ark in the Metz Synagogue after its recapture.*

**above** *Men of the 5th Infantry Division, US Third Army, break down a door to a house on a street in Metz. The French fortress city was defended stubbornly by both Wehrmacht (Regular Army) and Volkssturm (Home Guard) troops. It finally fell to the Allies on the 22nd.*

*A Red Army commander reveals the next day's plan of attack to Soviet infantry and tank crews gathered round a bonfire somewhere in East Prussia.*

The French commander of a US M3 half-track gives a mock Nazi salute to the cameraman as his vehicle enters the centre of Strasbourg on the 27th. To add to the ridicule a crew member has placed a portrait of Adolf Hitler on the front of the vehicle. A young resident of the city takes the opportunity to pose for the same photograph by leaning on the mudguard of the half-track.

The commander of a Sherman of the US Ninth Army gestures to the vehicle following his to halt, as the ground ahead is too muddy for tanks. This photograph shows clearly the appalling weather conditions that the Allies faced in their drive to push back the Germans over the Rhine into the Reich.

Mrs C. Ashurst of Eccles, Manchester, takes a break from welding parts for landing craft in Brocklebank shipyard, Liverpool. Mrs Ashurst became a war worker after her husband had been killed on active service. Women played a vital role in keeping Britain's war effort going whilst most able-bodied men were away in the armed forces.

An RAF corporal with his Alsatian dog 'Jett' searches the remains of a house for survivors after a V1 attack in southern England. The early war German blitz had taught the emergency services the value of finding trapped survivors quickly. To this end the RAF trained a number of police dogs in this ability.

Polish troops fought alongside the British in the 21st Army Group. Polish forces were responsible for liberating the Dutch industrial centre of Breda at the end of the month. The town was one of the last German strongholds on the southern side of the Maas river. Here Polish forces assemble in the centre of the town before pushing north.

**below** On the 16th King George VI visited the Naval Combined HQ to view the operations room, where the cross-Channel landing operations for D-Day were directed. After the invasion the centre was used to control the supply convoys making their way from Britain to France.

A British 'Tommy' on sentry duty looks out toward the enemy from his billet on the front line, a deserted German café, on the 30th.

A Platoon of the 1st Battalion the Middlesex Regiment holds the left flank of the 15th Scottish Division, a large cabbage field, north-east of Liesel, Holland, on the 2nd.

On Armistice Day, 11 November, a special ceremony was held in the Forest de Compiègne, site of the signing of the German surrender in the First World War and of the French capitulation in 1940. To Hitler the German defeat was a great humiliation and when the opportunity arose he gleefully took revenge, insisting that the French sign the surrender in exactly the same railway carriage as had the Germans in 1918. Later the carriage was taken to Germany where it was put on public display. French boy scouts led a torch-light procession to the site where the carriage had been, and a symbolic ceremony of purification took place. This was the first time Armistice Day had been observed in France since 1939.

**below** The atrocious weather not only affected the progress of the Allied ground advance, it also seriously affected the ability of the RAF and USAAF to support the drive into Germany. Here RAF armourers struggle with a trolley load of bombs on a waterlogged airfield near the front line.

Frances Day, a famous singer of the day, has a drink during the interval of her show in Brussels on the 24th. She toured the theatres of the liberated towns and cities along with comedian Will Hay, raising the morale of the troops.

The Women's Royal Naval Service (WRNS) carried out many important roles during war time. Here two women members of a crew of a ship's boat, used to ferry between the shore and large vessels anchored out at sea, wake first thing in the morning with a cup of tea.

On the 23rd, US servicemen, no matter where they were, celebrated Thanksgiving with a traditional turkey dinner. Over 30 million pounds of turkey were shipped from America to the men overseas. Here infantry in the front line near Geilenkirchen, Germany, eat their turkey only a few yards from the battle.

# DECEMBER 1944

# *Operation Autumn Mist*

WESTERN FRONT. Germany. During the first week of the month the Allies were busy preparing for large-scale offensives on all fronts.

Dec 2. With the fall of Dreisbach, Patton's US Third Army had cleared the west bank of the Saar river. That night the US 90th Infantry Division crossed the river near Dillingen and the 95th Infantry Division crossed opposite Saarlautern.

3. British troops captured Blerick, the last enemy-held town on the west bank of the Maas river. French troops at the southern end of the Allied line converged on the Colmar pocket, the last remaining German stronghold in France. Soon the Allies would be in a position to launch a massive offensive into the heart of Germany itself. In Italy a large offensive was planned to commence on the 3rd in an attempt to liberate Ravenna and Bologna.

4. The 13th Corps of the US Ninth Army had secured all of the area west of the Ruhr river except for the villages of Wurm and Müllendorf. The 95th US Division had captured most of Saarlautern and elements of the 5th US Armoured Division had reached Brandenburg. Taking advantage of the bridgehead over the Saar at Saarlautern, the US 20th Corps pushed over as many units as it could. Soon troops were fighting in the outskirts of the next major town, Fraulautern. The fortifications in this area formed part of Hitler's Siegfried Line, the last major defence line before the heart of the Reich.

Over the next few days the US 20th and 12th Corps opened offensives in order to break through the defences and open a path into the German interior.

6. Units of the US 90th Division secured a bridgehead near Patchen, while troops of the US 95th Division continued to fight for Saarlautern, Fraulautern and Ensdorf. The 6th Armoured Division and 35th Infantry Division of US 12th Corps meanwhile managed to establish themselves on the eastern bank of the Saar between Grosbliederstraff and Wittrin. American troops were now fighting in the heart of the Siegfried Line along a front of several dozen miles.

10. The Germans launched a counter-attack to push the American forces in the Patchen–Dillingen bridgeheads back across the Saar. The Americans only managed to hold on with great difficulty. The German attack failed and the US foothold inside the Siegfried Line was secured.

Belgium. 16. The Allied success in breaking into the Siegfried Line was soon overshadowed when 250,000 German troops from the 7th and 15th Armies and the 5th and 6th Panzer Armies launched 'Operation Autumn Mist' in the Ardennes at the juncture between the US First and Third Armies. The 'Battle of the Bulge' had begun.

Hitler's objective was to split the Allies, slicing through

# DECEMBER 1944

their lines, retaking the Channel port of Antwerp. This would leave the British 21st Army Group stranded to the north of the German salient. This, it was hoped, would force another 'Dunkirk' for the British, trapped without a supply source. It might even lead to a negotiated peace and the dismemberment of the US/British Alliance.

The offensive opened at 5.30 a.m. on a front between Monschau and Echternach in the Ardennes area. Facing thirty German divisions were six American divisions of General Leonard T. Gerow's 5th and General Troy H. Middleton's 8th Corps, many of them green troops who had recently entered the front line for the first time. The attack took the Americans completely by surprise, units holding the front simply collapsing under the onslaught.

When news finally reached Eisenhower at Allied HQ he immediately dispatched the US 82nd and 101st Airborne Divisions to the area in an attempt to stem the German advance. This proved vital, as the 101st, with their heroic stand in the besieged town of Bastogne, were eventually to frustrate German hopes of opening a road net that would continuously supply their advancing forces.

Allied air power was unusable in the winter conditions, all planes being grounded by dense fog. The German counter-offensive went well at first, the Allies falling back in disarray. However, the 101st Airborne, recently arrived in the town of Bastogne, held out, even when surrounded by numerically superior enemy forces. Bastogne commanded the road net through which German supplies would have to move if the offensive were to be successful.

22. The Germans asked the surrounded Americans to surrender and received the one word answer 'nuts' from General Anthony C. McAuliffe, commander of the besieged garrison. When they asked for clarification McAuliffe stated that it meant 'go to hell'.

23. The skies cleared for the first time, enabling the Allied Air Forces to give much-needed support to the troops on the ground. German supply columns using a very restricted road net, due in part to the 101st's stand at Bastogne, became easy targets for the roving Allied aircraft. The Germans, desperately short of petrol and relying on captured American supply dumps, lost most of their home-produced supplies in this way. The advance began to slow. Field Marshal Gerd von Runstedt, the German commander in the west, had already foreseen this and had requested on the previous day that he be allowed to suspend the offensive and withdraw to the Eifel mountains. Hitler forbade any retreat, his eyes still firmly fixed on Antwerp and the splitting of the Allies. It had become clear to all the German field commanders that this objective had now become impossible to reach.

25. General Hasso Freiherr von Manteuffel's 5th Panzer Army was the only one making any sustained forward progress. The offensive halted sixty miles from its start line, near Dinant on the River Meuse. The Allies were driving into the Ardennes salient from both north and south.

26. Tanks of the 4th Armoured Division, part of Patton's US Third Army, broke through to the besieged defenders

*Members of the US 101st Airborne Division sing 'Silent Night, Holy Night' at Midnight Mass, Christmas Eve, in the besieged town of Bastogne. The night itself was anything but silent, the town being under constant shellfire. A few minutes after this photograph was taken, the Luftwaffe joined in, bombing the area, leaving their own Christmas message.*

**opposite** *A Stuart light tank covers a group of US infantry as they attempt to recover an abandoned jeep whilst under enemy fire on the edge of the Ardennes salient in Luxembourg on the 22nd.*

of Bastogne. The 'Battle of the Bulge' continued on into January 1945, but as a fighting withdrawal by the Germans rather than an offensive that might effect the outcome of the war in the west.

**MEDITERRANEAN.** Italy. 3. The British 8th Army opened its offensive towards Bologna with three Corps, the 2nd Polish on the left, the 5th in the centre and the 1st Canadian along the Adriatic coast.

4. Units of the Polish 2nd Corps liberated Montecchio, whilst troops of the Canadian 1st Corps entered Ravenna. Over the next few days the offensive slowed as German resistance stiffened.

9. The offensive was finally abandoned.

13. The British 6th Armoured Division began an attack on Tossignano.

14. The Polish 2nd Corps resumed its attack towards Bologna. On its right the British 5th Corps advanced on Faenza, the 2nd New Zealand Division soon reaching the River Senio.

17. Several small bridgeheads had been established across the Senio by troops of the 10th Indian Division.

21. The 5th (Kresowa) Division of Polish 2nd Corps had cleared the east bank of the Senio in their sector, while the Canadians reached the river near the Adriatic coast. This was however where the offensive ended. Fresh troops

to continue with the push were not available, those currently in the line were too exhausted to carry on. On the US 5th Army front the Germans began an attack of their own.

26. However the Allies, forewarned by Enigma intelligence, had reinforced the area, with the 8th Indian Division in the Serchio Valley. After initial gains the Germans were pushed back and the Allies undertook the offensive. By the end of the month they had regained all territory lost in the assault.

Greece. 3. An uprising began in Athens, now under British military jurisdiction. ELAS, the Greek Communist Party, was attempting to set up a state modelled on Tito's Yugoslavia to the north. British troops intervened to put down the insurgency and a battle for the control of the city began. Stalin, true to his earlier agreement with Churchill, withheld all aid from the communist forces.

28. The British government did not wish to become embroiled in a lengthy civil war and Churchill arrived in the capital on a surprise visit to broker a peace deal between ELAS and the recently installed government. The fighting continued even while the negotiations took place.

**EASTERN FRONT.** The Soviets continued to steadily push back the German forces throughout the month.

3. Troops of the 2nd Ukrainian Front captured Miskolc, north-east of Budapest, a key position in the German defensive line and an important industrial centre.

5. Soviet forces of the 3rd Ukrainian Front reached the shores of Lake Balaton to the south of Budapest.

**opposite** *Two grimy and weary members of the US 101st Airborne Division take a break from the front line in the besieged town of Bastogne. The strain of days of unending combat can be seen etched into their faces.*

**opposite below** *Three members of a Waffen SS patrol dash across a road on the first day of their counter-offensive in the Ardennes on the 16th. In the background can be seen abandoned and burning US guns and vehicles.*

*Men of a US field artillery battalion (left to right: Private G. F. Morris of New York, Private S. B. Holmes of Saginaw, Michigan, Private J. Coleman of Raymond, Massachusetts and Corporal Namiss Terry of New York) dig in along the main highway west of Bastogne to make a stand against the German counter-offensive. The US Army was a segregated force with black troops being kept in separate units from white fellow Americans. The establishment took the racist view that the black soldier was unreliable and could not be trusted in the front line, hence their relegation to secondary duties, such as drivers and engineers. It was not until manpower shortages forced the US authorities to form black American combat units that they were able to show their true worth. On the whole black American troops performed just as well as their white counterparts, many of them fighting and dying for the Allied cause in the last months of the war. It is interesting to note that the British Army held no such prejudices. Black Britons who joined the forces were fully integrated into normal combat units from the very beginning, many serving with distinction throughout the war.*

6. The German High Command admitted for the first time that Russian troops had managed to cross the Danube to the south of the Hungarian capital via Csepel island. Things looked grave for the defenders of Budapest.

As well as facing the Red Army in Hungary, the Germans were now fighting several different nationalities. Rumanians were engaged against them in the north of the country, while Bulgarians and Yugoslavs were fighting in the south against Army Group F, which was steadily pushed back.

9. The Bulgarian government announced that its troops had completed the occupation of Serbia and Macedonia, previously held by units of German Army Group E.

15. Soviet forces established a bridgehead across the River Ipley, gaining a foothold in Czechoslovakia, the last of the countries under German domination.

17. Russian troops had reached to within five miles of Budapest. Hitler, determined that the city should not fall, transferred several divisions from Germany and Italy to bolster the defence of the city.

24. The Soviet Supreme Command announced that in the course of the past three days the 3rd Ukrainian Front had advanced twenty-five miles, capturing the towns of Szekesfehervar and Biske. The Germans' escape route from Budapest was now less than eighteen miles wide. Two days later troops of the 2nd and 3rd Ukrainian Fronts linked up. Budapest was now totally surrounded.

27. The bitter street fighting for Budapest began, the 2nd Ukrainian Front attacking from the east of the city and the 3rd Ukrainian Front advancing from the west. Two

Soviet soldiers (one a Hungarian communist) were shot dead as they attempted to negotiate a surrender while carrying a white flag of truce. This ensured that the Russians would show no mercy to the remaining defenders. The battle for Budapest was to be a brutal and bloody one.

AIR. The RAF and USAAF continued to attack synthetic oil factories and depots throughout the month. This was having a devastating effect on the German war machine. A decoded telegram sent by the Japanese ambassador to Tokyo underlined Germany's problems when he reported that with only 300,000 tons of oil being produced each month the Germans were having great difficulty keeping their tanks on the move and their planes in the air.

On the 26th, as part of the offensive against Germany's oil industry, US bombers attacked the synthetic oil plant at Monowitz. By accident a bomb fell on the death camp at Auschwitz killing five SS guards.

During December, despite the dismantling of the gas chambers by the Germans, 2,093 Jewish women were murdered in Auschwitz. The full horror of Hitler's 'Final Solution' would soon become apparent to the people of the world, as Allied troops were now only a few miles away from many of these concentration camps.

The head of Bomber Command, Sir Arthur Harris, continued to insist that the crippling of Germany's war industry would only be successful if the German people's morale was also broken. To this end he continued to demand that significant Allied bomber resources be given

A group of thirty-three German soldiers, dressed in American uniforms and driving captured US vehicles infiltrated enemy lines just before the start of the Ardennes counter-offensive. The men, all able to speak perfect English and led by famed SS Colonel Otto Skorzeny, caused havoc behind the US lines by changing road signs, destroying bridges and telephone wires and selectively assassinating unfortunate soldiers in the US rear. This not only disrupted the US command and communications system but created an air of mutual suspicion amongst the troops on the ground. General Omar Bradley, commander of the US 12th Army Group was stopped at gunpoint three times by nervous GIs who demanded he prove who he really said he was! Fifteen of the commandos were eventually caught by the Allies and shot as spies. Here Officer Cadet Gunther Billings is tied to a post before being executed by firing squad.

**opposite** The initial success of the German counter-offensive in the Ardennes can to an extent be explained by the bad weather which grounded the Allied air forces. Here American A-20 Havoc bombers of the US 9th Air Force attempt to take off during a fierce snowstorm to give ground support to troops in the 'bulge' area.

Antwerp was not the only Continental city to suffer bombardment by Hitler's terror weapons. V1 flying bombs were launched at other towns in the Low Countries after their recapture by the Allies. Here US soldiers tend to Dutch civilians injured in an explosion when a flying bomb fell on the outskirts of their village on the 15th.

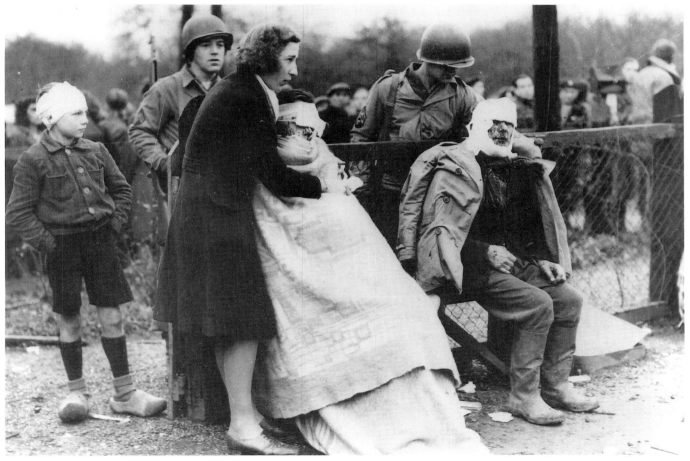

over to the attacking of German cities, despite the evidence that these resources might be put to better use elsewhere.

On the 5th, 282 Lancasters and 10 Mosquitoes attacked the German city of Heilbronn. Virtually unopposed by the Luftwaffe, over 2,000 tons of incendiaries were dropped on the city. Over 7,000 civilians died. Twelve Lancasters were lost.

The RAF also continued with its attacks on targets such as Gestapo HQs and SS prisons. On the last day of 1944 British Mosquito aircraft attacked the Gestapo HQ in Oslo. Although the building was destroyed there were innocent civilian casualties. A tram passing nearby was hit by a stray rocket; only four of its passengers survived.

HOME FRONT. The 3rd saw the disbanding of the Home Guard, which had been brought into being during the dark days of 1940. Contingents from all over Britain took part in a farewell march past through the centre of London, the salute being taken by King George VI.

On the 9th, the blackout was in effect lifted, as instructions were given that windows no longer need be curtained should an air-raid siren be sounded. This did not mean that attacks on Britain had stopped. Hitler's V weapons continued to fall, 367 people being killed and 847 wounded by explosions in December. These casualties were not confined to London. On the 28th, German aircraft launched V1 flying bombs against the north of England. In Oldham twenty-eight people, including a woman of seventy and a six-month-old child were killed in a single blast.

British casualties from V1 flying bombs and V2 rockets were light when compared with the deaths caused by these indiscriminate weapons in Antwerp. On the 16th, the first day of the German Ardennes offensive, a V2 rocket landed on a packed cinema killing 567 people, 296 of them Allied servicemen on leave from the front. On the 21st, sixteen people were killed when a rocket landed on a hospital. The next day another rocket landed on exactly the same spot killing three workers sifting through the rubble for survivors. In all, 3,752 Belgian civilians and 731 Allied servicemen were killed by V weapon attacks on Antwerp that winter. The city suffered more casualties under Allied occupation than it had lost in the battle for its liberation four months earlier.

**opposite** *Soon after their arrival in Greece British troops found themselves embroiled in a civil war between right-wing forces who supported the return of the monarchy and the communists, influenced by the success of Tito's forces to the north in Yugoslavia. Here British paratroopers involved in the street fighting in Athens attempt to winkle out communist snipers in the city centre.*

**this page** *A tank crewman of the 8th Hussars dashes across a street known to be under enemy observation on Christmas morning. It only becomes apparent why he is risking himself in the next photograph in the series. A few doors away men of the same unit eat their Christmas Dinner with a jug full of rum!*

When the Germans blew up a dyke near Arnhem on the 2nd, a large area of land to the south-east of the town was flooded. The Canadian 2nd Corps was forced to withdraw from its bridgeheads over the Waal river. Movement was not only restricted but was always in view of enemy positions on surrounding higher ground. Here on the 14th an infantry platoon is forced to go on patrol by boat.

A sergeant of the Kings Dragoon Guards examines a sign chalked on the side of one of the unit's vehicles in Italy on the 1st.

Five days before Christmas a group of infantrymen draw for the right to receive home leave. A lucky few were able to see in the New Year at home with their loved ones.

**opposite** The first three aircraft of a large formation of B-17 Flying Fortresses release their bombs over the rail installations at Bergen on the 29th.

Christmas Day in the front line. Rifleman Corker, 1st Battalion the Rifle Brigade, from Muswell Hill, enjoys a Christmas pudding in his foxhole near Nieuwstadt.

*A group of West Indian servicemen and women broadcast home on the BBC Overseas service on the 26th as part of a programme of greetings and entertainment for the citizens of the British Empire.*

*Corporal S. Maughan, Flight Sergeant F. Best and Leading Aircraftsman J. W. Ambridge of the RAF 2nd Tactical Air Force decorate one of the bombs to be dropped over the German lines on Christmas Day. All three were on duty throughout Christmas Eve preparing hundreds of aircraft to go on bombing missions the next day.*

Glen Miller addresses the troops on ABSIE (American Broadcasting Service in Europe), giving information about his forthcoming tour of Europe. During the summer of 1944 Miller and his American Band of the Allied Expeditionary Force had played throughout Britain, often with such guest vocalists as Bing Crosby and Dinah Shore. In November the orchestra had been ordered to move to France where they could entertain troops much nearer the front. The band made the crossing without incident. Glen Miller set out from England by air on the 15th, a foggy day which had grounded all other flights. His plane never arrived in Paris. No wreckage was ever found. It was later assumed to have crashed somewhere in the English Channel.

Christmas was livened up by the shows of famous entertainers, keeping up the morale of the troops. Here Bob Hope mingles with the audience at one of his performances in London during the festive season.

The crew of a Soviet 45 mm anti-tank gun prepare to shell enemy positions in a Hungarian village during their offensive to the Danube.

A panoramic view of a Soviet attack in progress somewhere in Poland. Infantry were often used in this rather primitive fashion, frontally assaulting enemy positions without regard to casualties. As a result the life expectancy of a Russian soldier was shorter than in any other Allied army.

The Red Army suffered from a severe lack of motorized transport for its infantry. Soviet infantrymen often found themselves riding into battle on the back of tanks. Here soldiers leap from T34s as they seize another objective in their encirclement of Budapest.

# JANUARY 1945

# *Winter Offensive*

WESTERN FRONT. Belgium. Jan 1. The 3rd and 8th Corps of Patton's US Third Army continued to slice into the base of the German salient in the Ardennes, with the liberation of Moircy, Jenneville and Chenogne.

2. German troops of Army Group G continued with their offensive in Alsace, advancing on the town of Bitche, fifteen miles to the south-east of Saarbrucken.

Strasbourg was not to be abandoned, its defence being taken over by troops of the 1st French Army. General de Gaulle had threatened to withdraw French forces from the front line had the city been allowed to fall to the Germans. Eisenhower agreed to garrison the city on the condition that French troops would defend it if necessary.

5. Troops of the 553rd Volks Grenadier Division established a bridgehead over the Rhine some twelve miles to the north of Strasbourg.

12. Fierce fighting continued in the Strasbourg sector. The French 3rd Algerian Divison held off repeated German attempts to reach the city.

20. The US Seventh Army in Alsace were holding their ground. A significant amount of territory had been lost to the Germans, but not Strasbourg. The battle cost the Americans 16,550 dead and the Germans approximately 25,000.

France. 1. In Alsace, the southern sector of the Western Front, units of German Army Group G under General Hermann Balck (some ten divisions) launched 'Operation North Wind', in an attempt to throw back General Alexander M. Patch's US Seventh Army and recapture Strasbourg. Under orders from Eisenhower, US forces retreated to a defensive line on the crest of the Vosges mountains. This potentially meant abandoning the capital of Alsace to the enemy.

2. A further three Ardennes towns, Gerimont, Mande St Etienne and Senonchamps were recaptured by units of the American 8th Corps. Manteuffel, Commander of the 5th Panzer Army, requested that he be allowed to withdraw his forces to Houffalize. Hitler once again refused. The army was now in danger of becoming cut off, if the Allied units advancing into the base of the salient from north and south linked up. The Führer justified his order on the grounds that with the Allies occupied with reversing German advances into their territory, they are in no position to launch a major attack into the Reich itself.

3. The US First Army began a major push to reach Houffalize in the Ardennes 'Bulge'. At the same time Manteuffel ordered a last desperate attack on Bastogne with the aim of cutting the corridor to the town. The attack

*The congregation was killed when a V2 rocket landed on this church on Sunday the 16th in a town in the south-east of England.*
**opposite** *Its starboard engine ablaze, an A-26 Invader of the 9th US Air Force heads for its base at Munstereifel after attacking its target, a rail junction behind the Ardennes 'Bulge' in early January. The aircraft's bombs can be seen exploding in the lower right hand corner of the photograph.*

succeeded in halting the Allied drive into the salient for twenty-four hours but did not break the link between Bastogne and the outside world.

4. The British 2nd Army launched its first offensive of the New Year against German forces remaining on the west bank of the Ourthe. At the same time, in the Ardennes, Hitler gave permission for the 6th SS Panzer Division to be withdrawn from the salient and transferred to the east, where a massive Russian offensive was expected.

6. In the Ardennes, units of the US First Army linked up with troops of the US Third Army on the road between Manhay and Houffalize. The salient was now much reduced although no significant numbers of enemy troops had been cut off. The withdrawal of the 6th SS Panzer Division had made the German position even more vulnerable. It was now only a matter of time before they were back on their start line of 16th December. Over the next few days American forces continued to push German troops back.

8. General Manteuffel ordered the withdrawal of much of his force from Houffalize to a wooded ridge five miles further east.

10. The British 51st Highland Division attacking south into the salient liberated St Hubert, making contact with the 7th Corps of the US Third Army attacking to the north.

12. The Americans recaptured Amberloup, Lavacherie, Fosset and Sprimont. The German 7th and 5th Panzer Armies retreated steadily in all sectors of the salient.

13. British 30th Corps ends its participation in the 'Battle of the Bulge' when it reached its objective, the River Ourthe south of Laroche.

14. The US 17th Airborne Division relieved the 101st Airborne at Bastogne. Units of the 101st were still engaged with the enemy to the east of the town, between Noville and Rachamps.

15. The British launched a limited attack to capture Bakenhoven. This was in preparation for their upcoming winter offensive, 'Operation Blackcock', to clear the German pocket between the Meuse and the Ruhr south of Roermond.

16. The German salient in the Ardennes had been reduced to half its former size, running from Monschau in the north, south via St Vith and Houffalize, then southeast to Wiltz and Ettelbruck and finally on to Echternach.

17. In the course of 'Operation Blackcock' units of the 7th Armoured Division captured Echt and Susteren. The next day 12th Corps entered Schilberg and Heide. The German defenders, men of the 1st Parachute Army, were however making the going extremely tough for the British.

20. The German forces in what remained of the Ardennes salient prepared to retire back to their former defensive positions inside Germany.

21. US troops recapture Crendal, Lullange, Hoffelt, Hachville and Wiltz. 'The Battle of the Bulge' was now over, with almost all of the territory lost having been regained. Over the next few days, with an improvement in the weather, Allied aircraft hammered the retreating German columns attempting to cross the River Our back to their original defensive positions. The battle cost the Americans 75,000 and the British 4,000 casualties. The Germans, however, lost well over 100,000 men in addition to 800 irreplacable tanks and 1,000 aircraft.

24. British troops taking part in 'Operation Blackcock' captured Haaren (52nd Division) Montfort (7th Armoured Division) and Schleiden (43rd Division).

25. Linee, Putbroeck and Kirckhoven were captured.

26. The operation closed, the German bridgehead between the Meuse and the Ruhr having been eliminated.

Germany. 29. The US Third Army resumed its winter offensive against the Siegfried Line, the 90th Division crossing the River Our and capturing the towns of Wachenhausen and Staupbach. Over the next two days three US divisions, the 9th, 99th and 2nd, advanced into the German defence line. At the same time, further north, the US 18th Airborne Corps crossed the German border near Bucholz and the 78th Division, US Ninth Army, opened an offensive towards the Ruhr river.

MEDITERRANEAN. Italy. 1. An almost complete calm reigned over the whole Italian front. The lull in the fighting was to last for several weeks while General Clark planned his major offensive to break into the plains of northern Italy.

2. There was limited activity on the Senio as troops of the Canadian 1st Corps secured the river line in its entirety.

12. The Cremona Division, the first Italian unit to fight in the front line with the Allies, saw its first combat as part of the Canadian 1st Corps in the Alfonsine area.

EASTERN FRONT. Hungary. 1. In Budapest the fighting raged on, with the Russians making slow but definite progress in capturing the city.

2. German Army Group South attempted to break into Budapest from the north-west.

6. It was clear that the German attack on Budapest had failed. However, the Germans had recaptured Esztergom, an important position north-west of the capital.

**opposite** *After heavy snowfalls in early January, American troops found it difficult to patrol in some sectors. Several units improvised ad hoc solutions. Here a platoon of GIs venture forth on cross-country skis. They are led by a Norwegian serving in the US Army, who teaches them how to operate in this environment. The white smocks that the men wear are in fact requisitioned bed sheets.*

*Private G. Bryan of Birmingham and Private F. Holmes of West Bromwich distribute rations to the troops using an improvised goat cart to help them carry food across the slippery ground.*

Fighting continued throughout the rest of the month in Budapest. There was a further blow to the Germans when on the 20th the Hungarian government signed an armistice with the Soviet Union, Britain and the United States. The last remnant of the European Axis was now broken.

Poland. 12. As the battle for Budapest continued, Soviet forces opened their massive winter offensive in Poland. 'Operation Vistula-Oder' was started on the 1st Ukrainian Front, which advanced from the Sandomierz bridgehead towards Breslavia. On the same day, the 2nd Belorussian Front attacked with nine armies over the River Narew, north of Warsaw. The first of seven German defence lines on the Vistula was breached within twenty-four hours.

13. The advance continued at spectacular speed, the 47th Army of the 2nd Belorussian Front surrounding Warsaw.

14. Yet another offensive was opened by the Russians, with the 1st Baltic and 3rd Belorussian Fronts attacking in the area of Schlossberg in the north-east of East Prussia. In Poland the attack continued, with the 1st Belorussian Front obtaining a bridgehead over the Vistula and pushing on towards Radom and Lodz. The 1st Ukrainian Front captured Kielce, a strategically important railway junction.

15. The offensive became a general one all along the line when the 4th Ukrainian Front joined in with an attack into the Carpathians in the Sanok area.

16. Radom was captured by units of the 47th and 61st Armies. The speed of the Russian advance caught the Germans by surprise. Their lines ruptured, they retreated in disarray. Some units near to encirclement managed to fight their way free but many others were bottled up in pockets behind the Soviet advance. Many thousands of German troops found themselves trapped like those men in Budapest and Memel.

The 1st Belorussian Front advanced an average of twenty-five miles a day. The 1st Ukrainian Front progressed more than sixty miles in the first four days of the winter offensive.

18. The surrounded city of Warsaw was finally cleared of its last remaining defenders.

19. Soviet troops further north captured Schlossberg. Troops south of the capital capture Lodz and the 52nd Army liberated Krakow.

22. Russian troops crossed the border into Upper Silesia, attacking the important industrial and mining towns of Kronstadt and Strehlitz. The Soviet Armies were now quickly forging through the Reich itself. Over 2 million German civilians fled westwards towards Berlin.

25. General Hans Reinhardt, Commander of Army Group Centre in Poland, was dismissed after requesting that he be allowed to retreat to a defence line along the Masuri lakes. General Lothar Rendulic was given command. After his first examination of the situation he estimated that some thirty-five German divisions had so far been lost during the Russian offensive.

26. Troops of the 2nd Belorussian Front reached the Baltic between East Prussia and Danzig, and 500,000 German soldiers were cut off from Germany proper. On the same day another town, Hindenburg in Silesia fell. In Poland, Soviet forces surrounded the German fortress cities of Poznan and Thorn.

28. The Memel pocket trapped far behind the Soviet lines finally fell to troops of the 1st Baltic Front.

31. Russian troops managed to gain a foothold across the Oder at Zehden. This was the nearest they would get to Berlin for some time. On the same day the first four towns of Brandenburg (Landsberg, Schweibus, Miedzyrzecz and Zullichau) were captured by the Red Army.

CONCENTRATION CAMPS. Early in the new year the Allies began to liberate the first concentration camps used to hold political prisoners and those of 'undesirable' race, such as Jews and Gypsies. On the 3rd, the Allies revealed the location of a camp at Breendonck in Belgium. The horrors of this camp, although many, were however to pale into insignificance when, on the 26th, Soviet troops liberated the death camp at Auschwitz. The Germans had done their best to destroy the gas chambers and leave as little evidence as possible of the mass extermination of the Jewish people that had taken place there. Russian soldiers found 648 unburied corpses and more than 7,000 starving and skeletal survivors. The liberators also discovered the charred ruins of twenty-nine enormous warehouses. A further six had survived attempts by the retreating Germans to set them alight. Inside were found 836,255 women's dresses, 348,000 men's suits and 38,000 pairs of men's shoes, a small proportion of the belongings of the hundreds of thousands of Jews put to death in the camp.

**opposite** A South African Beaufighter of the Balkan Air Force fires its rockets at an enemy HQ in the town of Zuzemberk, northern Yugoslavia.

**right** A flight sergeant and lieutenant at RAF HQ update their map of North West Europe, following the progress of Allied land forces. Most of the major cities fought over are marked. At the bottom of the map can be seen Saarlautern, scene of heavy fighting as the US Third Army forced its way through the Siegfried Line. Level with the knees of the lieutenant on the ladder is the 'Bulge' area, gradually being recaptured by Allied forces. Bastogne and Houffalize are clearly marked. Troops of the US First Army, under British command, continue to push north-west from Aachen (level with the top of the ladder) and troops of the 2nd British Army push into Germany from Holland (the area above the lieutenant's papers pinned to the map).

**opposite** *British troops were better prepared for the onset of winter than were their American allies. Instead of bed sheets British infantrymen were issued with specially designed snow smocks to allow them to blend in with their surroundings. They were also issued with helmet and gun covers so that as little kit as possible was left showing against the snowy background. Here a patrol probes the enemy front line, near Gangelt, Germany on the 11th.*

**right** *Corporals James Quaranto and Joseph Smith, both of the US 26th Infantry Division, work their way through the ruined outskirts of Wiltz, Luxembourg. The town, near the base of the Ardennes salient, had been one of the first to fall to the German counter-offensive. Its recapture signalled the end of the the 'Battle of the Bulge'.*

**below** *A US heavy machine-gun crew keep a sharp lookout toward enemy lines, Banigne, Luxembourg, on the 11th. Their chosen vantage point is not very inconspicuous, as they attempt to take some cover from a frost-covered tree on a hill's crest line.*

A Sherman tank of the 75th Infantry Division, whitewashed and covered
in snow to help in its camouflage, speeds towards the village of
Commanster to the south-west of St Vith in the Ardennes salient.

A 57mm gun and crew of 1st Platoon, 333 Anti-Tank Company, US 83rd Infantry Division, cover a snow-covered, tree-lined road near Bovigny, half-way between Houffalize and St Vith in the Ardennes salient.

Two snow-covered German soldiers surrender to British troops near Hongen on the 20th. Note the youth of these soldiers. Allied forces were beginning to capture regularly teenagers of sixteen or younger fighting in the ranks of the Wehrmacht.

A Vickers machine gun of the 8th Battalion, Middlesex Regiment, gives supporting fire to an infantry attack on the 8th. The semi-permanent nature of the dugout and the empty belts of ammunition and discarded cartridge cases tend to suggest that this position has been held for quite some time.

Italian troops, equipped and trained by the British, went into action for the first time against their former allies on the 12th. Here a mortar team from the Cremona Division fires on a German strong point in the town of Alfonsine.

*A machine-gun post at night on the 1st Ukrainian Front, somewhere in East Prussia.*

*These photographs, both taken on the 10th, show Soviet infantry fighting their way through the streets of Budapest.*

# FEBRUARY 1945

# *Through the Siegfried Line*

WESTERN FRONT. France. Feb 1. The French 1st Army continued to attack the Colmar pocket.

2. The French 5th Armoured Division entered Colmar, still being stubbornly defended by German troops.

3. Colmar was liberated by units of the French 1st Army, which then pushed south and east from the town to clear the last remnants of German forces from French soil.

5. What remained of the Colmar pocket was cut in two as troops of the US 21st Corps linked up with French forces moving south from the town.

7. French forces in Alsace reduced the Colmar pocket to four villages west of the Rhine.

9. All German resistance in this sector came to an end. Apart from several ports on the Atlantic coast that had now been cut off for several months, all of France was free from German occupation. The German 19th Army had been all but destroyed in the fighting, losing some 25,000 men.

Germany. 1. The Canadian 1st and American Ninth Armies put the finishing touches to their preparations for Operations 'Veritable' and 'Grenade'. The Canadian objective was to clear German forces from between the Maas and Rhine rivers, whilst the Americans were to attack across the River Ruhr towards the Ruhr area, the industrial heartland of Germany.

In the US First Army sector units of the 5th Corps pressed on towards the dams on the Ruhr and Urft rivers. Further south the 8th Corps of the US Third Army battered its way through the Siegfried Line, capturing the towns of Manderfeld, Auw, Mutzenich and Winterscheid.

2. The 1st and 82nd Divisions of the US First Army opened their own offensive into the Siegfried Line.

3. The first US units crossed the Ruhr at Dedenborn, preparing a bridgehead from which troops could strike towards the Schwammenauel Dam.

5. The offensive towards the Schwammenauel Dam began, units of the US 78th Division leading the attack.

6. US troops in the First and Third Army sectors continued to break into the Siegfried Line. The fortifications were strong but American firepower gradually weakened German resistance. It was only a matter of time before the defence collapsed and a path into the interior of the Reich was opened.

7. The US 78th Division, pushing towards the Schwammenauel Dam, captured the towns of Kommerscheidt and Schmidt. On the same day German forces defending the dam opened its floodgates to try and stem the US advance. This was just what the Americans hoped to avoid. The flood waters crashing down the Ruhr severely

disrupted the First and Ninth Armies' planned crossing, scheduled to take place over the next few days.

8. 'Operation Veritable' began. The attack started at 10.30 a.m. after an intense air and artillery bombardment. Taking part were all four divisions of the British 30th Corps. They quickly pushed south, overcoming resistance from the German 1st Parachute Army, reaching Kranberg in the Reichswald forest after the first day of operations. The next day the advance continued rapidly, with Mehr, Niel and Millingen all captured. The first breach of the Siegfried Line by British troops was achieved when the 15th Scottish Division took the Materborn heights.

10. The Germans opened a counter-attack in the Cleve area in an attempt to push the British back from the Siegfried Line. Large areas of land had been flooded to try and slow the British and Canadian offensive. The counter-attack, allied with the flooding, stalled the advance of three of the four divisions taking part. The Germans, however, did not have the strength to push the British back and after some reorganization the offensive was resumed.

12. Within two days the British were advancing once again, attacking enemy positions in Cleve and Materborn. The Canadian 3rd Division had reached Kellen and the 15th Scottish Division was pushing on around Cleve towards Calcar. The 43rd Wessex Division captured Bedburg, whilst the 51st Highland and 53rd Divisions advanced through the Reichswald forest.

13. The resistance of the German 84th Division in the region was finally overcome.

The 3rd Corps of the US First Army began to take up positions along the west bank of the Ruhr in preparation for an assault crossing. Activity along the US Army's front reduced. After a month of hard combat to break into the Siegfried Line many of the units were completely exhausted. However, the Allied forces were now in a very strong position to exploit their breakthroughs at several points. The German Army was extremely short of reinforcements and was unable to fill the gaps with sufficient troops of a high enough quality to stop a co-ordinated Allied offensive.

15. A new corps, the 2nd Canadian, was added to 'Operation Veritable'. Its role was to clear the area around Calcar, which it did with speed and efficiency.

17. Units of 30th Corps were at the outskirts of Goch.

18. The town was attacked by three British divisions, the 15th (from the north) the 51st (from the north-west) and the 43rd (from the east).

20. The offensive was resumed against the Siegfried Line by units of the US 8th Corps. They penetrated the line north of the town of Dahnen. In the US Third Army sector there was also a general resumption of offensive operations, the 80th Infantry and 10th Armoured Divisions advancing into the Siegfried Line south of Mettendorf, between the rivers Our and Gay.

In the area of operations of the Canadian 2nd Corps only two wooded hills, the Hochwald and Balbergerwald

*Royal Navy MTB (Motor Torpedo Boat) 378 patrols a stretch of Adriatic coast north of Ravenna, still in the hands of the Germans, although few of their ships ever venture out into the open sea.*
**opposite** *Soviet infantry clear the Budapest suburbs of German resistance during the first week of February.*

remained in German hands. Field Marshal Gerd von Runstedt asked permission to withdraw what little was left of the German forces to the east bank of the Rhine. Hitler replied that every centimetre of German territory must be defended to the last man.

23. The US Ninth Army launched the delayed 'Operation Grenade' across the Ruhr river. Its objective was to clear the area between the Ruhr and Rhine of enemy forces in preparation for a major offensive across the Rhine itself planned for March. The attack began at 3.30 a.m. with units of the US 13th and 19th Corps crossing the river by boat. The Germans were taken by surprise and gave ground rapidly. To halt this, Hitler ordered the Panzer Lehr and 15th Panzer Grenadier Divisions to the area to reinforce the defenders and throw the Americans back across the river. At the same time troops of the US First Army also crossed the Ruhr near Duren. Further south the US Third Army crossed the Our and the Saar with units of the 12th and 20th Corps.

24. Units of the Canadian 1st Army continued with their mopping up as part of 'Operation Veritable'. The British 53rd Division advanced from Goch towards Weeze.

Meanwhile 'Operation Grenade' was making steady progress. The US 84th Division captured Doveren and the 29th Division completed the capture of the fortress town of Julich. The 30th Division entered Hambach and Niederzier in the early hours of the 25th.

25. 'Operation Grenade' continued, with the 35th Division and 5th Armoured Division of the US Ninth Army crossing the Ruhr opposite Linnich. In the US First Army sector Düren was captured by units of 7th Corps. The offensive by the US Third Army in the south continued with an equal amount of success, units of the 4th Armoured Division establishing a bridgehead over the river Nims at Rittersdorf.

The areas between the Maas and the Rhine were clear of the enemy. British and Canadian forces then began their build up for a massive attack across the Rhine which was planned to take place in March.

26. The Canadian 2nd Corps opened 'Operation Blockbuster' to clear the towns of Calcar, Udem and Xanten. Taking part were two armoured divisions, the Canadian 4th and the British 11th, and three infantry divisions, the Canadian 2nd and 3rd and the British 43rd.

27. The Canadian 2nd Corps continued with 'Operation Blockbuster', the Canadian 4th Armoured Division penetrating into the Hochwald forest. The Canadian 3rd Division reached Udem and the British 11th Armoured Division approached Kervenheim.

In the US First Army sector units continued to make progress on the plains west of Cologne. The 10th Armoured Division and the 76th Infantry Division advanced on the city of Trier.

29. Advance units of the Canadian 2nd Corps concluded their participation in 'Operation Blockbuster' by reaching their objectives on the west bank of the Rhine. In the US Ninth Army sector the advance over the Ruhr continued with the 29th Division pushing on towards München-Gladbach. The 2nd Armoured Division reached Neuss, only five miles from the Rhine. In the US Third Army sector troops of the 20th Corps continued to push towards Trier. The Siegfried Line was now well and truly breached.

Substantial numbers of Allied troops had broken through the fortified lines and across the formidable river barriers that lay in their path. Several major German cities were now within reach. Only one barrier, the Rhine, remained before the Allied troops.

**MEDITERRANEAN**. Italy. During February there was once again only very limited Allied activity. General Clark was only willing to open a major offensive when the worst of the winter weather had abated. There were limited operations in the early part of the month along the western coast by the US 92nd Division. This was to improve Allied positions in preparation for the spring offensive.

25. Further Italian units took their place in the front line alongside Allied troops. The Folgore Division, previously an élite parachute unit of Mussolini's Italian Army, took over the sector of the front previously held by the 6th British Division.

Greece. 12. The civil war in Greece came, at least temporarily, to a close. The talks instigated by Churchill in December had at last come to fruition and the communists agreed to suspend their military action pending further negotiations.

**EASTERN FRONT**. Baltic. 3. Soviet forces of the 1st Baltic Front attempted to eliminate the large pocket of troops trapped in Latvia but were repulsed by the fanatical defenders. Preparations were under way to evacuate as many of these troops as possible by sea to Germany itself. However, now that Russian submarines were based in Finland, it was becoming ever more dangerous for ships packed with refugees and soldiers to traverse the Baltic.

Further south, in the besieged port of Königsberg, German destroyers gave naval gunfire support to the beleaguered defenders. Transports took off 184,000 trapped refugees.

Poland. 1. The Soviet offensive continued. Russian troops opened the siege of the German fortress city of Poznan, now several miles behind the front line. At the same time the Red Army continued to advance on the Oder, the last major river line before Berlin.

5. Soviet troops reached the Oder, only thirty miles from Berlin, pressing to the north and south of the fortified city of Küstrin. Attacks continued on the besieged city of Poznan.

7. Troops of the 1st Ukrainian Front crossed the Oder near Frankfurt. Further north, isolated units of the German Army still held on to various towns, amongst them the strategically important port of Elbing. However, they were not to hold it for much longer.

10. Troops of the 1st Belorussian Front captured the important railway junction at Eylau, while troops of the 2nd Belorussian Front seized the port of Elbing. The garrison of Arnswalkde was surrounded but rejected Russian offers of surrender.

11. Russian forces broke through the German lines north and south of the chief city of Silesia, Breslau. The city's 150,000-man garrison was now in danger of encirclement.

15. The ring around Breslau finally closed, and yet another German-held city was surrounded by the Russians. The Red Army also captured the encircled town of Sagan. Fortunately for the Germans they were able to extricate the town's defenders, the Hermann Goering Corps.

19. Breslau was now under sustained attack. The fighting continued through the remaining days of February with the Russians making steady if slower progress. German resistance seemed to be stiffening now that the Fatherland's capital was under direct threat.

22. Poznan, the fortress city behind the Soviet lines in which Hitler placed so much faith, finally fell. Out of 60,000 defenders only 12,000 remained alive at the end of the siege.

At the end of the month the Germans managed to form an *ad hoc* defence line running roughly along the length of the Oder. Significant German forces held out in fortress cities, such as Königsberg, far to the Soviet rear, and a balcony of land along the northern edge of the Baltic was still held by them. However, they did not have the men or the equipment to hold off another sustained offensive by the Red Army. The last reserves of the Wehrmacht were gathering near Lake Balaton, south of Budapest, to put in the last major German attack of the entire war.

Hungary. 1. Desperate fighting raged in Budapest as German strong points were methodically eliminated.

7. Russian troops fighting their way into Budapest managed to capture the railway station, a former German strong point.

**opposite** *Two British soldiers keep a sharp lookout from their cleverly disguised dugout on the River Senio, Italy.*
**right** *Dirty and bearded GIs of the US Third Army take a break from the front line in a captured German pillbox near Prum on the 12th.*

**above** A US infantry company practise river-crossing assaults on the 22nd in the few hours before the real thing, when they will be sent against enemy positions across the River Ruhr.

**left** Men of a US infantry patrol dash up a street in Duren under enemy fire on the 23rd.

**above** A British soldier on the Dutch-German frontier on the 14th reads a sign warning him to be vigilant in enemy territory.

**below** A line of Canadian Buffalo amphibious carriers wait on the Nijmegen to Cleve road during 'Operation Veritable'. Note the floods which made this sort of vehicle invaluable to the advancing Allies.

British infantrymen take cover behind an M3 half-track on the outskirts of Cleve. Note the Nazi party eagle drawn on the house in the background. It was a common occurence during the last months of the war for the German authorities to paint heroic slogans and devices on to prominent buildings in the hope that this would encourage the inhabitants to fight just that little bit harder.

Private M. Bain, an infantryman of the 51st Highland Division from Fort Augustus, Scotland, pulls down a swastika flag from a window in Cleve on the 13th.

10. The 2nd Ukrainian Front made large advances in its attempts to clear Budapest.

11. Forty-five city blocks fell to the Red Army.

13. The city fell after a 45-day siege. About 135,000 Germans were taken prisoner. Some units attempted to fight their way out of the city to the German 8th Army, but only 7 officers and 120 men escaped through the lines of Marshal Rodion Malinovsky's 2nd Ukrainian Front.

Balkans. 7. German troops began to evacuate Mostar and other areas of northern Yugoslavia. This was in order to shorten the German front line and release more troops to face the Russian onslaught in Hungary and Poland.

18. By this day many of the troops of German Army Group E had been evacuated from Yugoslavia and transferred straight into the front line in Hungary. However, the severely weakened forces at the extreme southern end of the German line seemed to be holding their own under attack from Yugoslav and Bulgarian forces.

At the end of the month the last Wehrmacht reserves were gathering near Lake Balaton, south of Budapest, for the Germans' last major attack of the war.

AIR. The Allies continued with their bombing campaign, attacking both industrial and civil targets. On the 1st, Berlin was subjected to a heavy RAF bombing raid. This was to be the first of many aimed at the capital through the month. On the raid of the 3rd, amongst the 1,000 Germans killed, was Roland Friesler, President of the People's Court which had presided over the trial and execution of the Germans involved in the plot to assassinate Hitler.

On the 11th and 12th record-size raids were launched against Essen and Dortmund, as 1,079 and 1,108 bombers raided the cities with 5,000 and 5,487 tons of bombs respectively.

Then, on the 13th and 14th, the Allies carried out the most devastating raid of the entire war on the German city of Dresden. The raid was ordered after a request by the Soviets to destroy the rail yards in the city. The operation was however made a general one to bomb the entire city. The head of Bomber Command, Sir Arthur Harris, was still convinced that the direct bombing of the German population was a war-winning tactic, despite all the evidence to the contrary.

Two waves of RAF Lancasters, the first of 245 planes, the second of 550, dropped tens of thousands of incendiary bombs on the almost completely undefended city. It was obliterated in a giant firestorm that burned for four days and nights. The following day, even as the fires were still raging, a further 450 USAAF bombers attacked the city again. The exact number of victims is unknown, estimates of the casualties varying between 130,000 and 200,000 (of which 60-70,000 were deaths). Only eight aircraft were shot down in the entire operation. In comparison, British air-raid casualties for the entire month of February were 483 killed and 1,152 wounded. The bombing of Dresden was the most pitiless Allied bombing operation of the Second World War. The city was of little strategic or military

*Private Bill Watkins of Taunton, Somerset, covers the advance of two comrades as they dash across 'sniper's corner' in Goch on the 23rd. Private Watkins carries a Panzershreck, the German equivalent of the Bazooka.*

**right** *A group of British infantry mock the likeness of Hitler they have discovered in a house in Cleve on the 14th.*

importance. Even Winston Churchill criticized the raid: 'The destruction of Dresden remains a serious query against the conduct of Allied bombing.'

The Allied bombing in February did not end there. On the 22nd 'Operation Clarion' was launched, a massive bombing campaign by 10,000 aircraft to attack transportation lines inside the Reich. Two hundred individual targets were attacked, with bombers coming in over their targets as low as 5,000 feet to ensure the accurate delivery of their payloads. These raids once and for all ended the German's ability to move units on any significant scale within the Reich.

The WVS (Women's Voluntary Service) continued throughout early 1945 collecting household goods for bombed-out families in the London area. Here a woman gives over some of her unwanted kitchen untensils at a WVS collection point in St Pancras.

**opposite above** B-17 Flying Fortresses over their target. On the 14th, in a daylight raid, 450 USAAF aircraft attacked Dresden as the city still burned from the RAF raid of the night before.

**opposite below** A panoramic view of the ruins of Dresden after the firestorm raid of the 13th/14th.

**below** Air Chief Marshal Sir Arthur Harris examines aerial reconnaissance photographs at his High Wycombe HQ. 'Bomber' Harris was the most fervent advocate of area bombing, where civil populations as well as industrial targets were attacked.

# MARCH 1945

# *Across the Rhine*

WESTERN FRONT. March 1. British troops continued with their advance in the Kervenheim sector and through the Hochwald and Balberg forests. The town of Venlo fell to the US 35th Infantry Division and München-Gladbach was captured by troops of the US 29th Infantry Division. This was the most important German city to fall so far to the advancing Allies.

2. Troops of the British 53rd Division captured Weeze, the last town in the so-called 'Roermond triangle'. This area had been significantly reduced by last month's 'Operation Veritable'. In the US Ninth Army sector troops of the 83rd Division reached the Rhine opposite Dusseldorf but found that all bridges across the river had been blown.

4. In the Canadian 1st Army sector, the 43rd Wessex Divison thrust south towards Xanten while two other divisions, the Canadian 2nd and 3rd, completed the capture of the Hochwald and Balberg forests. The British 53rd Division captured Geldern and linked up with the 35th Division of the US 16th Corps. Troops of the Ninth US Army mopped up the last pockets of resistance in the Cologne plain to the west of the city, while troops from the US First Army began to probe at the city's defences.

5. Units of the US 5th Armoured Division reached the Rhine at Orsoy. The US 19th Corps captured Reinhausen,

eliminating all German resistance on the western side of the Adolf Hitler bridge. This completed the last of the tasks assigned to troops in 'Operation Grenade'. The attack on Cologne was opened by the US 3rd Armoured Division from the north in the early hours of the morning. The US 104th Infantry Division continued its advance on the western and southern outskirts of the city.

6. The British 43rd and Canadian 2nd Divisions prepared for a set piece assault on the town of Xanten, while the British 53rd Division continued to advance towards Wesel, an important objective on the east bank of the Rhine. At the same time 'Operation Grenade' was offically ended on the US Ninth Army front. Troops of the US 3rd Armoured and 104th Infantry Divisions continued with their attacks on the city of Cologne, fighting their way through the city street by street.

7. The city, Germany's third largest, finally falls to two of the three divisions of US 7th Corps (104th Infantry and 3rd Armoured). Its other division, the 9th Armoured, continued with its advance to the south of the city, managing to capture a bridge across the Rhine at Remagen. German engineers attempted to blow the bridge as US troops made a rush for it but the main charges failed to detonate. It was the only bridge still standing over the river. General Bradley

*Soviet Guardsmen attack a German strong point somewhere in East Prussia.*

**opposite** *'Able' Company, 71st Regiment, 44th Infantry Division, US Seventh Army cross the River Neckar on the 30th in an attempt to seize Mannheim on the far bank. The city stands at the junction of the Rhine and Neckar rivers.*

immediately ordered that every available man in the sector be pushed across. The capture of the bridge was a blow to Hitler, who had hoped that the Rhine would provide an insurmountable obstacle in the Allies' path. As a direct result of its capture Field Marshal von Runstedt was dismissed from his command as head of German Forces in the West and was replaced by Field Marshal Albert Kesselring, recalled from Italy.

8. Over the next two days, the US 3rd Corps, holding the bridge, was attacked constantly by German artillery and aircraft. More than 300 Luftwaffe planes, including nearly all of their available jets, bombed the bridge but failed to collapse it into the Rhine.

10. Over the next few days German forces withdrew over the Rhine, blowing all the other bridges after they had crossed. Bonn was captured by troops of the US 1st Division. The Rhine had been reached by Allied forces along almost its entire length. 'Operation Blockbuster', launched the previous month, came to an end with the capture of the Calcar–Xanten–Uden sector. The total cost in casualties to the Allies of this and 'Operation Veritable' was 7,300 American, 5,500 Canadian and 10,500 British troops.

12. The Americans had held off a series of counter-attacks by the German 7th Army against the Remagen bridgehead. In the US Third Army sector all resistance east of the Rhine had been brought to an end. The heavy fighting between the US 3rd Corps and the German 7th Army had however meant that the Americans were unable to move out of their bridgehead with the speed they had first hoped to attain. Nevertheless a significant amount of the German Army was tied up while it should have been manning defences up and down the east bank of the Rhine.

15. The US Seventh Army operating to the south of the American line launched 'Operation Undertone' with the objective of clearing a pocket of land between the Rhine, Moselle and Lauter-Saar rivers.

16. Units of the US 8th Corps launched their planned assault across the Moselle, sending two regiments over in the area between Willingen and Kolber.

18. The advance of the US 3rd Corps across the Remagen bridgehead continued with the capture of the town of Windhaven and a line of hills along the River Weid. Units of the US 87th Division opened their attack on Koblenz, whilst the US 89th Division established a bridgehead over the Moselle in the Wittlich area. All formations of the US Seventh Army continued with 'Operation Undertone', hoping to complete their task before the opening of the planned offensive over the Rhine.

23. The 21st Army Group began 'Operation Plunder', the massive Allied offensive across the Rhine north of the Ruhr. The Canadian 1st Army crossed north of Emmerich, the British 30th Corps opposite Rees and the 12th Corps near Wesel.

24. Some 3,000 aircraft and gliders carrying 14,000 paratroops of the British 6th and American 17th Airborne

On the 8th a V2 rocket fell on Smithfield Market in central London, killing 110 people, most of them market workers. Here a badly wounded woman is stretchered away by rescue workers and police.

**opposite** A phosphorous grenade explodes in the midst of a US patrol in Cologne on the 7th. Although intended primarily as a smoke-producing weapon, the phosphorous grenade could cause severe chemical burns to people unlucky enough to find themselves in the blast radius.

Divisions landed their troops north-east of Wesel. These quickly linked up with the troops forging across the Rhine. By the evening, the British 2nd Army had established a bridgehead some six miles deep on the east bank.

25. The offensive of the US 7th and 3rd Corps continued between Cologne and Remagen. The 7th Corps of the US Third Army opened its attack across the Rhine, sending the 87th Division to the east bank between Braubach and Bopard. The 60th Division, after crossing the Rhine near Oppenheim, headed for the River Main and Frankfurt.

26. Units of the British 30th Corps succeed in extending their bridgehead over the River Ijssel. The 6th Armoured Division of the US Third Army reached the south bank of the Main and attempted to push into the city. However, German resistance was very tough.

27. As the British 2nd Army continued its advance east of the Rhine, north of the Ruhr the US Ninth Army advanced to its south. A huge pocket was in the process of being formed, potentially trapping thousands of German troops in the industrial heart of the Reich.

28. The British Army began its advance on the Elbe in central Germany. The 80th Infantry Division of the US 20th Corps attacked across the Rhine and the Main simultaneously, taking a firm bridgehead in the Mainz sector. At this point the Allied front line runs south along the Rhine, with large salients on the eastern bank as far as Haltern on the River Lippe in the north and as far as Marburg, Giessen and Wiesbaden in the south.

29. The Canadian 2nd Corps continued to meet strong resistance in the Emmerich area, but the British 8th Corps

pushed on rapidly towards Osnabrück. In the US First Army sector, Frankfurt finally fell to troops of the 5th Infantry Division.

30. Emmerich was captured and the US Third Army pushed on toward Usingen and Butzbach. Fighting continued around Mannheim between the US 15th Corps and the German 1st Army.

31. The Allied advance on the east bank of the Rhine continued at a rapid pace. The French 1st Army opened their own offensive across the Rhine in the Speyer and Germersheim area at the southern end of the Allied line.

**MEDITERRANEAN. 2.** On the Italian front the Cremona Division, supported by Partisans of the 28th Garibaldi Brigade, opened an offensive against Comacchio. At the same time a limited attack was begun by the 4th Corps of the US Fifth Army in the mountains against Monte Torraccia and Monte Castello. The British 56th Division established a strong position on the opposite bank of the Senio near San Severo.

5. These limited offensives were brought to a close. There were few other offensive operations in the rest of the month.

**EASTERN FRONT. Poland. 1.** The German Vistula Army Group evacuated its bridgehead over the Oder in the Schwedt area. Fighting flared up in the areas of East Prussia still held by the Germans, as the Red Army attempted to frustrate their effors to evacuate its troops back to the Reich.

2. Over the next few days the Germans managed to hold off concerted attacks across the Oder.

5. The Soviets completed the capture of Stargard and Naugard, the forts to the south-east of the important Oder town of Stettin. As a response to the ever-increasing disparity in numbers on all fronts, Hitler announced that fifteen-year-old boys would in future be drafted straight into the ranks of the German Army.

9. The Russians smashed through the defences of Küstrin and bitter house-to-house fighting developed. The 2nd Belorussian Front pressed on towards Danzig.

12. The 1st Belorussian Front captured the fortress town of Kustrin, one of the major bastions on the road to Berlin. In East Prussia the 3rd Belorussian Front split German forces around Königsberg, reaching the coast to the south-west of the port.

18. The 1st Belorussian Front captured the town of Kolberg in Pomerania, the last German strong point between the Polish corridor and Stettin on the Pomeranian coast.

20. Soviet troops took Dabie Aldamm in Pomerania, wiping out the last remaining German bridgehead on the east bank of the Oder. They made steady progress over the next few days, breaking down the German defence lines that had crystallized along the west bank.

28. By this date the Russians had wholly captured the port of Gdynia and managed to enter the west part of the port of Danzig.

30. The whole of Danzig was in Russian hands. In Silesia the Red Army continued with the liquidation of the defences surrounding the fortress towns of Glogau and Breslau.

Hungary. 6. The Germans launched 'Operation Wildtaufel', their last major counter-offensive of the war. The offensive north and south of Lake Balaton had as its objective the eventual recapture of the Hungarian oil-fields. Ironically, lack of fuel was a decisive factor in the outcome of the counter-attack. Initially it went very well, the lead elements of Army Group E inflicting heavy casualties on the Bulgarian 1st and Yugoslav 3rd Armies. South of Lake Balaton, the German 2nd Armoured Army's attack was contained by the Russian 27th Army only after giving several miles of ground between Lakes Balaton and Velencei.

10. Marshal Fyodor Tolbukhin, commanding the Soviet forces in the area of the German counter-attack, requested reinforcements. He was told he must manage with the troops already available. Meanwhile, the Germans poured in their last armoured reserves along the Sarviz Canal, west of Lake Velencei. So far they had managed penetrations of twenty miles into the Soviet lines.

12. The thrust between Velencei and Balaton stalled. Hitler was so angry that he ordered the Liebstandarte Adolf Hitler Division to lose all the privileges it had gained as his élite bodyguard. Soviet forces went over to the offensive again, and also began to attack in Yugoslavia.

25. By this date the German defence line was crumbling, with troops of the 3rd Ukrainian Front advancing over thirty

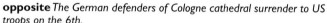

**opposite** *The German defenders of Cologne cathedral surrender to US troops on the 6th.*
**above** *A portrait of Adolf Hitler lies amongst the ruins of an art gallery in central Cologne on the 6th.*
**above right** *A US Army padre hears the confession of a GI before he returns to the front line near Aversmacher.*

miles in one day towards the Austrian border. More and more sectors of the German front dissolved into cauldron battles with forces attempting to fight their way west to where they might be able to make another stand.

29. Units of the 3rd Ukrainian Front entered Austria. The Russians also captured the towns of Szombathley, Koseg and Kapuvar. Bitter fighting continued behind many sectors of the front, where small German Kamfgruppes (battle groups) were still attempting to fight their way back to friendly areas.

30. As the 3rd Ukrainian Front advanced into Austria, German Army Group E was in increasing danger of being cut off from the Fatherland.

**AIR.** The Allies continued with their bombing campaign throughout the month.

2. American bombers once again attacked the marshalling yards at Dresden.

14. The Biefeld railway viaduct was attacked by the RAF's new 10-ton bomb carried by specially converted Lancaster bombers.

15. American bombers dropped 1,300 tons of explosives on the German Thorium ore plant at Oranienburg. German atomic bomb research was brought to a complete halt.

18. Massive air attacks were launched against Berlin and Frankfurt, the raid on the latter city involving over 1,200 aircraft. Over a thousand civilians were killed in each raid. The German air force committed its last reserves of jet fighters against the raids, shooting down twenty-four Allied bombers and five fighters.

21. Between now and the 24th the RAF launched a series of raids against Berlin in an attempt to draw Luftwaffe reserves from the area around the Rhine, where they could hamper the Allied ground offensive. On the 21st, eighteen RAF Mosquitoes launched a low-level bombing attack on the Shell Petroleum HQ in Copenhagen. Three floors of the building contained records on the activities of the Danish Resistance. On the top floor the Gestapo had imprisoned thirty-two Resistance fighters. In the basement more Danish citizens were being held and tortured. So only the middle three floors had to be hit. They successfully completed their attack and only six of the freedom fighters on the top floor were killed. Over one hundred Germans died in the attack. The rest of the prisoners managed to escape and were smuggled out of Copenhagen to Sweden.

22. The RAF completed a week-long bombing campaign in support of British and American ground forces. Allied aircraft flew 21,692 missions throughout Europe.

30. US Air Force bombers sank ten German submarines in the Bremen–Hamburg area.

HOME FRONT. This month saw the last German attacks on British soil in the Second World War.

5. East Anglia was attacked by twelve Luftwaffe bombers, although very little in the way of damage or casualties was achieved.

3. The Germans launched the first V1 flying bombs against London since the previous September. Twenty-one missiles were fired from aircraft. Seven of them reached the London area.

27. The Germans fired the last V2s of the war from their one remaining launch site near The Hague. One of the rockets fell on a block of flats in Vallance Road, Stepney, and killed 134 people. Late in the afternoon, at Orpington in Kent, a single man was killed by another explosion. He was the last civilian casualty in Britain.

31. British air-raid casualties for March were 792 killed and 1,426 wounded. In total the 1,115 V2s launched against Britain had claimed the lives of 2,855 people.

*Throughout the war the Royal Navy escorted convoys of merchant ships full of vital supplies to the north Russian ports of Murmansk and Archangel. Here the Flower Class Corvette HMS Honeysuckle, of convoy JW65, ties up next to the aircraft carrier HMS Trumpeter in the Kola inlet on the 21st. Note the thick ice covering the sea's surface even as spring is taking hold on almost every other front.*

**opposite above** *British troops cross the tributary of the Maas during their attack on Weeze on the 2nd.*
**right** *Men of the 7th Armoured Division rush an enemy strong point while covered by one of their comrades, Stadtholn, Westphalia, on the 31st.*

**opposite above** *A Bofors anti-aircraft gun of the US Third Army stands in front of the Opera House in the main square of Frankfurt. The city, sixteen miles east of the Rhine was captured on the 29th.*

**above** *Troops of the US Ninth Army, part of the British 21st Army Group, train for the Rhine crossing on the River Maas a day or two before the real thing, which took place on the 23rd/24th.*

**opposite below** *Leading Aircraftsmen W. Meadows of Nottingham and I. J. Davies of St Davids load rockets on to a RAF Typhoon ground attack aircraft at a forward airfield.*

**opposite** *A US soldier on reconnaissance examines the Ludendorff railway bridge across the Rhine on the morning of the 7th. As the Americans approached the bridge, the Germans attempted to destroy it with pre-positioned demolition charges but these failed to destroy the spans across the river. Within hours troops of the US First Army had gained their first foothold on the eastern bank of the river.*

**opposite below** *After the Ludendorff rail bridge at Remagen was captured it came under sustained attack from the Luftwaffe, who tried to stop the Americans taking advantage of the only bridge standing over the Rhine. Here quad 20 mm anti-aircraft guns mounted on half-tracks cover the approaches to the bridge on the 8th.*

**above right** *British infantry climb out of an assault boat on the east bank of the Rhine on the 24th.*

**right** *British Royal Marines of the 1st Commando Brigade crossed the Rhine at 10 p.m. on the 23rd. By 2 a.m. their first objective, the town of Wesel, had been entered and 350 prisoners taken. Here British commandos man Vickers machine guns in the ruins of Wesel on the morning of the 24th.*

**below right** *Soon after the first British tanks had crossed the Rhine on the 24th they linked up with US paratroopers dropped behind the German lines. Here men of the US 17th Airborne Division hitch a ride on the back of a Churchill tank of the Guards Armoured Brigade in the town of Appelhulsen as they head towards Munster some nine miles away.*

**below** *As Allied forces pushed on through the Reich they began to come across camps which had been used to hold slave labourers, forcibly taken from Eastern Europe to work in German war industries. By mid-March freed workers were arriving at reception centres near Paris at the rate of over 2,000 a day. Most of them were suffering from severe malnutrition. Here a Russian boy tucks into a feast of bread and molasses, the first meal he has had for several days.*

*C-47 Dakotas drop a second wave of paratroopers and supplies over their drop zones on the east bank of the Rhine on the morning of the 24th.*

*Sergeant Greenley of the 21st Independent Parachute Company (the Path-finders) awaits the order to take up his position at the door of an aircraft over Germany on the 24th. Sergeant Greenley was the first paratrooper to land in the whole Rhine crossing airborne operation, being the lead man in the first 'stick' to be dropped.*

*Paratroopers descend from their aircraft during the opening hours of the attack across the Rhine on the 24th.*

# APRIL 1945

# *The Collapse of the Reich*

WESTERN FRONT. After the Allies had crossed the Rhine and breached the last defence line before the German interior, it was only a matter of time before the Third Reich came to its end. As the Allies advanced into Germany the combat rapidly became isolated encounters against *ad hoc* battle groups protecting various military installations and population centres. Towards the end of the month Allied forces were encountering resistance mainly from groups of die-hard SS or Volkssturm (Home Guard) pensioners and young boys. German war industry had ground to a halt, the artillery had run out of shells and vehicles were unable to move from lack of fuel.

Apr 1. The month began with the Canadian 2nd Corps extending and reinforcing its Emmerich bridgehead and the British 8th Corps widening its foothold on the east bank of the Dortmund–Ems Canal.

The US First and Ninth Armies linked up at Lippstadt, closing the circle round the industrial region of the Ruhr, trapping the whole of Model's Army Group B and two corps of the 1st Parachute Army.

Units of the US 19th Corps reached the Berlin-to-Cologne autobahn. This system of roads, built by the Nazis in the 1930s, the most modern in the world, was to speed up the Allies' advance through the heart of Germany.

2. The Canadian 1st Corps advanced from its Nijmegen bridgehead towards Arnhem, scene of bitter fighting the previous September during 'Operation Market-Garden'. The British 8th Corps continued with its advance on Osnabrück.

3. In the Ruhr area the US 18th Airborne Corps came into the line. Together with units of the US 3rd Corps they slowly began to eliminate the Ruhr pocket. At the same time the British consolidated their hold across the Dortmund–Ems canal. Units of the 8th, 12th and 30th Corps had now established themselves along this barrier.

The US 80th Division fought its way into Kassel, which was tenaciously defended by units of the 7th German Army. On the same day Aschaffenburg surrendered to the US 45th Division after three days of heavy fighting. The US 21st Corps began its attack on Würzburg.

4. On this date and the 5th, British troops pushed on across the Dortmund–Ems canal and headed for the River Weser. Meanwhile, units of the British 8th Corps entered Osnabrück. American forces continued with their attacks into the Ruhr pocket. Further south troops of the US Seventh Army captured Germunden and units of the US 21st Corps completed the crossing of the Main near Würzburg.

**above** *Four Liberator B-24 aircraft of the US 15th Air Force on their run in to target, early April, northern Italy. Two of the planes have been hit by flak and are losing height and smoking.*

**opposite** *Leading Aircraftswomen Petronella Burke of Winchelsea and Hilda Collins of Uddingstone were the first WAAF (Women's Auxiliary Air Force) drivers to serve on the Continent after D-Day. Here they consult their road maps as they learn to navigate their way around occupied Belgium.*

7. The British 8th Corps had completed its crossing of the Weser in the Minden area against little resistance. Further south the US 84th Division did the same.

8. Units of the British 30th Corps began to attack the defensive positions of the 1st Parachute Army east of Lingen and to push on towards the city of Bremen. American troops crossed the Leine south of Hanover and the French 1st Army took Pforzheim and established a bridgehead across the River Enz near Mühlhausen.

9. Units of the US 13th Corps opened their attack on Hanover from the north and west of the city. Meanwhile British troops continued with their advance into northern Germany east of Lingen.

11. Both the British 12th and 8th Corps were across the Leine and Aller rivers, pushing on towards Bremen, only meeting with sporadic resistance. The US 16th and 18th Airborne Corps advanced deeper into the Ruhr pocket, crossing the Ruhr and Sieg. To their south the US 20th Corps neared Weimar and the German extermination camp at Buchenwald.

12. The 1st Corps of the Canadian 1st Army opened its assault on Arnhem. The penetration of the Ruhr pocket proceeded at a fast pace, large numbers of German prisoners being taken. In the British 2nd Army sector, 30th Corps continued its attack towards Bremen while the 8th Corps advanced on Uelzen. On the same day Franklin D. Roosevelt died at Warm Springs in Georgia after a long illness. The Vice-President, Harry S. Truman, took over the running of the American war effort.

14. The US 18th Airborne Corps began the last stage of its offensive into the Ruhr pocket. The US 3rd Corps, also fighting in the area, completed the capture of the areas assigned to it.

15. Arnhem was finally liberated, whilst further south the US Seventh Army continued with its offensive in the Nuremberg and Neustadt sectors. Meanwhile the French 1st Army occupied the Black Forest, the 1st Corps crossing the Rhine near Kehl.

16. Units of the British 30th Corps reached the outskirts of Bremen and troops of the 8th Corps fought their way

into Uelzen, meeting heavy resistance from units of the German 20th Army. On the same day troops of the US 14th Corps reached the suburbs of Nuremberg. Units of the US 9th Armoured Division liberated the famous prisoner-of-war camp at Colditz. The US 69th Division pushed on north-east towards Leipzig.

The Allied offensive had now penetrated into the heart of Germany. Many areas now being liberated by the advancing Americans were to be in the Soviet zone of control after the war and eventually form part of East Germany. The Allies' advance became ever more rapid against less and less opposition. The fiercest fighting was farther east where German units were desperately trying to hold back the Russians whilst in effect waiting to be taken prisoner from behind by the advancing western armies.

17. Units of the British 30th Corps had entered Bremen and were fighting their way through the city. The US 19th Corps began its assault on Magdeburg on the west bank of the Elbe river. Now that Eisenhower had decided that the prize of Berlin would be left for the Russians, the Elbe had been made the demarcation line between the furthest points of the Allied advance from west and east. By the time the Western Allies reached the river, Soviet forces were still quite some distance away and many American units raced on further east.

In the Ruhr pocket the 18th Airborne Corps continued with their offensive, capturing the towns of Duisberg, Dusseldorf and Werden. Resistance was diminishing every day. Many German units were now giving themselves up without a fight. The corps had captured over 20,000 prisoners a day in the mopping-up operations. The US 2nd and 9th Divisions were approaching the outskirts of Leipzig whilst the US 14th Corps began its battle for Nuremberg. This city, in many ways the cultural centre of Nazism, where Hitler had held his great rallies since the 1930s, was staunchly defended by fanatical SS and Wehrmacht troops.

18. The Canadian 1st Corps reached the Zuider Zee, the final objective in their advance. The British 30th Corps prepared to launch its final offensive against Bremen. Soltau and Uelzen were captured by units of the British 8th and 12th Corps.

In the Ruhr pocket the Allies finished off the last of the German resistance. In total, since the beginning of the operation, they have taken 325,000 prisoners, more than twice the number of German troops at first thought to be trapped inside the pocket. Halle was captured by the US 3rd Division, while in the 5th Corps sector the US 2nd and 69th Divisions launched a co-ordinated attack on Leipzig. The US 42nd Division captured the town of Furth, encircling Nuremberg where a fanatical German defence still held on.

19. British troops reached the Elbe for the first time when troops of the 8th Corps captured Lauenburg. The autobahn between Bremen and Hamburg was cut by units

of 12th Corps. Hamburg itself was now close to falling. Leipzig surrendered to units of US 5th Corps. In the French 1st Army sector the 2nd Corps pushed on towards Stuttgart whilst the 1st Corps began to emerge from the Black Forest.

20. Nuremberg fell to a co-ordinated attack by the US 42nd, 45th and 3rd Divisions. The 7th Corps prepared to attack the city of Dessau at the confluence of the Elbe and Mulde rivers. On the same day Adolf Hitler celebrated his fifty-sixth birthday in his Berlin bunker.

21. The US 15th Corps advanced towards Munich whilst troops of the US 21st Corps headed for the Danube. Units of the French 2nd Corps captured Stuttgart.

22. Realizing at last that the war was lost, Himmler, head of the SS, approached the Red Cross to pass on a message to the Western Allies offering surrender but stating that the German Army would continue to fight on against the Soviets. Hitler knew nothing of this plot.

The same day US troops crossed the Danube near Dillingen. The French 1st Armoured Division also reached the river and began to advance in the direction of Ulm.

23. British forces reached the Elbe opposite Hamburg. The whole of the Dessau area was now under American control and the US 6th Corps continued its attack across the Danube.

25. Units of the US Third Army were pushing towards the German frontier with Czechoslovakia. The US Seventh Army extended its crossing points over the Danube, capturing several more both north and south of Dillingen. Troops of the Soviet 5th Guards Army made contact with Americans of the US First Army at the town of Torgau, on the Elbe south of Berlin. Germany was now cut in two.

26. Bremen finally fell to units of the British 30th Corps. On the same day US forces crossed the frontier into Austria at the town of Lackenhausen. The US 20th Corps bridged the Danube south-west of Regensberg. Further south the US Seventh Army, already over the river, continued its advance in the direction of Augsberg.

27. Himmler received a reply from the Western Allies to his peace overtures: the Germans must surrender on all fronts. The US 12th Corps reached the Czechoslovakian frontier at Bischofsreuth. Regensberg surrendered to troops of the US 20th Corps.

29. The British 8th Corps crossed the Elbe in its last offensive operation of the war, the Baltic coast as its objective. This was to cut off the base of the Danish peninsula from the advancing Russians and stop them gaining a foothold in the country. The 15th Corps of the US Seventh Army opened its attack on Munich and captured several of its outer suburbs. Dachau concentration camp was liberated by US forces who were sickened at what they saw there.

30. Munich fell and the US 6th and 21st Corps pushed on to the Austrian frontier. The French 1st Army entered Austria in the vicinity of Bregenz. British troops continued with their offensive to reach the Baltic at Wismar.

MEDITERRANEAN. 1. In Italy the 2nd Commando Brigade launched 'Operation Roast' to capture the town of Comacchio in preparation for the planned spring offensive, due to be launched later in the month.

5. After the fall of Comacchio the US 92nd Division opened a limited offensive against the town of Massa. Again, this was to prepare a favourable position for the launching of the spring offensive in the US 5th Army sector.

9. The British 8th Army began its spring offensive in the evening. The British 5th and Polish 2nd Corps attacked in the Imola sector, whilst the British 10th Corps and Italian Fruili Combat Group launched an offensive across the Senio in the Lugo sector. The British 13th Corps stayed on the defensive at the left-hand end of the British line.

10. The US 92nd Division liberated Massa. The offensive by the 8th Army went well. Deception plans had made the German 10th Army expect an attack at the right-hand end of their line, not on its left where the offensive was now under way. By the 11th, the Polish 2nd Corps had reached the River Santerno.

12. The US Fifth Army offensive had to be postponed because of the bad weather. The Polish 2nd Corps was now over the Santerno and advancing at a rapid pace.

14. The weather had improved enough to open the US Army's offensive in Italy, the 4th Corps attacking Suzzano and Vergato. Later, during the night, the US 2nd Corps opened its offensive towards Bologna.

20. The US Fifth Army had fought its way through the Apennines and into the Lombardy plain beyond. The 4th Corps reaching Casalecchio only a few miles from Bologna.

In the British 8th Army sector the 10th Corps reached the River Idice. The German commander, General Heinrich von Vietinghoff, decided that a withdrawal behind the River Po was the only way he could re-establish his shattered front line. Unfortunately, Allied units had now interpenetrated the German defences to such an extent that an organized retreat was impossible.

21. The Polish 2nd Corps of the 8th Army and units of the American Fifth Army converged on Bologna. Troops from both now entered the city.

22. The US 4th Corps captured Modena, irretrievably breaking the German front line.

24. The US Fifth Army began to pursue the retreating Germans towards Genoa. The British 13th and 5th Corps succeeded in establishing bridgeheads over the Po. The Italian Partisan movement ordered a general uprising behind enemy lines.

25. Partisans took control of Milan. At the same time Verona was liberated by the US 88th Division.

26. Allied troops reached Genoa.

28. The US 1st Armoured Division reached Lake Como near the Swiss border. Units of 5th and 13th Corps of the 8th Army pressed on towards Venice.

29. The end of the war in Italy. At Caserta, Colonel Schweinitz and his adjutant signed the document on behalf of General Vietinghoff for the unconditional surrender of

*A Bren gunner of the 15th Scottish Division takes cover behind the Great War Memorial during heavy fighting in the centre of Uelzen on the 19th.*

all German forces in Italy, with effect from 1 p.m. Wednesday, 2nd May. Meanwhile, the Allied advance continued against little or no opposition. American troops entered Milan and British forces captured Venice.

30. Turin liberated by the US 92nd Division.

EASTERN FRONT. The battles were often fierce and bloody, as the Germans tried desperately to hang on to as much ground as possible. Many commanders viewed the resistance as gaining time for the Western Allies to capture large areas of Germany before the Soviets, thus preserving the Fatherland from the concerted pillaging and destruction that went on in areas captured by the Red Army. Hitler still believed that by some miracle the war could be turned around. This notion was to fade as the month went on.

Poland. Fierce fighting raged all along the front in the first days of April. The garrison of Breslau still valiantly held out while the surrounded troops at Glogau were ordered by German High Command to fight their way back to friendly lines. The last remaining ships of the German Navy, the cruisers *Prinz Eugen*, *Emden*, *Lutzow*, *Admiral Scheer* and *Hipper* evacuated 85,000 men and 70,000 wounded from isolated areas of the East Prussian coast and delivered them safely behind German lines in Pomerania.

6. Breslau still held out. In the Danzig area the Russians broke through the German 2nd Army's lines in several places. In East Prussia, the 2nd Belorussian Front opened a major attack on the besieged city of Königsberg. Some units managed to penetrate into the outer suburbs.

8. Fighting continued in Königsberg, Danzig and around the besieged fortress city of Breslau.

9. The garrison commander of Königsberg, General Otto Lasch, surrendered. A group of SS fanatics fought on for a few more hours inside the medieval castle but were eventually wiped out to a man. Hitler, hearing of Lasch's capitulation, ordered him to be shot as a traitor.

16. The artillery of the 1st Ukrainian Front signalled the beginning of the massive Russian offensive towards Berlin. By 7 a.m. Soviet troops had established themselves on the west bank of the Oder in significant numbers. At 6.15 a.m. the 1st Belorussian Front joined the offensive, advancing from the Küstrin bridgehead. Hitler sent his last ever order of the day to his Eastern Front forces: 'He who gives the order to retreat is to be shot on the spot.'

German forces still survived in several areas in East Prussia, but they were under constant air attack.

Austria. 3. Troops of the 2nd Ukrainian Front reached the plains around Vienna. German Army Group South was disintegrating, the Russians managing to maintain a daily advance of fifteen to twenty miles. There was fierce fighting on other sectors of the front, particularly around Bratislava, besieged by units of the 2nd Ukrainian Front.

6. The battle for Vienna began. All bridges across the Danube were blown except for one. The Russian 46th Army launched an outflanking manoeuvre to encircle the Austrian capital.

13. Vienna fell to the Soviets. German forces surrendered at 2 p.m. when it became clear that surviving units had become surrounded by troops from the 3rd Ukrainian Front. Meanwhile, the 2nd Ukrainian Front headed for St Pölten on the road to Brno in Czechoslovakia, an important arms manufacturing centre.

16. The position of the 6th SS Armoured Army grew more desperate by the hour.

Germany. 16. The battle for Berlin developed over the next few days. The biggest breakthroughs by the Red Army were made by the 1st Ukrainian Front over the Neisse. Army Group Centre gave ground but its lines were not as yet totally ruptured.

19. By now a large number of bridgeheads over the Oder had been won by the 2nd Belorussian Front. The 1st

Belorussian and 1st Ukrainian Fronts were across the Neisse and making steady progress. General Georgi Zhukov's forces were advancing rapidly towards Berlin from the Küstrin bridgehead.

23. Over one-third of the German defence line lay in tatters. Reconnaissance troops of the 1st Belorussian Front had already reached the outskirts of the German capital's eastern suburbs. Hitler took over direct control of the defence of the city. The city's garrison amounted to some 300,000 men. However, many of these were Volkssturm of little fighting quality, or policemen with little military training.

24. Forces from the Russian 3rd and 28th Armies, 1st Ukrainian Front, joined units of the 1st Belorussian Front attacking Berlin. The Belorussian Front pushed into the city from the east, the Ukrainian Front from the south. The fighting was bloody, with no quarter being given by either side.

Over the next two days Soviet troops made rapid progress westwards in other sectors of the front. They reached the Elbe and linked up with American forces advancing westwards. Fighting still continued in Breslau. Russian troops had managed to force their way inside the German defensive perimeter and the city was soon to fall.

27. Three-quarters of Berlin was in Soviet hands. The fighting was house to house, but the superior numbers and equipment of the Russians gave them a decided advantage. The German 9th Army desperately tried to fight its way through to the capital but was held by Red Army units in the vicinity of Zossen.

29. The fighting was focused around the Reichstag and the Chancellery, along the Potsdamerstrasse and in the Belle Alliance Platz. Only a few city blocks remained in German hands. The centre of Berlin had been reduced to a giant heap of rubble by the intense fighting. Hitler, realizing that the battle was lost, ordered that the war be continued from Nazi strongholds in the Bavarian Alps. He named Grand Admiral Karl Doenitz to be his successor as Head of State. He also married Eva Braun, his long-time mistress.

30. At 3.30 p.m. Hitler committed suicide in his Berlin bunker. His wife Eva Braun died alongside him. Even Hitler's pet Alsatian was put to death. The 9th Army had failed in its attempts to batter its way through to relieve the defenders of the capital. At 10.50 p.m. three assault battalions of the Russian 150th Infantry Division captured the Reichstag. During the night General Hans Krebs, Chief of Staff of the Wehrmacht, asked for negotiations to settle terms for the city's surrender.

The German Army had been half destroyed by the battles of the last month. Army Group South, 600,000 men strong, and Army Group Centre, containing 1,200,000 men, still continued to fight, not in an effort to defend the

*The Stars and Stripes is slowly raised over a Nazi eagle dominating the top of Hitler's dais in the Nuremberg Stadium on the 22nd. This vast arena had been the scene of many of the Nazi Party's great rallies before and during the war. At the top of the steps stand men of the 3rd Division, US Seventh Army. About to begin is a ceremony in honour of the division and its five recipients of the Congressional Medal of Honour (the American equivalent of the Victoria Cross).*

Reich but to hold off the Soviets and retreat into British and American lines where they could surrender with little fear of being shot or sent to Siberian labour camps.

**AIR.** The war in the air continued with large attacks on many German cities. On the 10th another heavy daylight raid on Berlin was mounted, 1,232 USAAF B-17s and B-24s taking part. The Germans tried to intercept the attack with Me-262 jet aircraft but the inexperience of their pilots told in the aerial dogfights. Fifty were lost to the bombers and their P-51 Mustang escorts for the loss of only ten Allied aircraft.

9. The RAF launched attacks on the last surviving remnants of the German Navy at Kiel. The cruisers *Admiral Scheer* and *Hipper* were sunk. The pocket battleship *Lutzow* was destroyed one week later in a follow-up raid.

On the same day Russian and RAF fighters co-operated for the first time, putting in joint attacks on German supply trains near Dresden.

At the end of the month the Western Allies began a different type of air operation when they launched a massive air drop of aid to the civilians of Holland still under German control. Reichskommissar Seyss-Inquart, in command of the region, agreed a temporary cease-fire in the air to allow this to take place. An estimated 3 million Dutch civilians were starving, the death rate from malnutrition rising dramatically. The area had been cut off from importing outside food supplies and what little was left was taken by the German Army.

**CONCENTRATION CAMPS.** The world first began to discover the real horror of Nazism. As the month went on camp after camp was overrun by the Allies and terrible scenes of death and suffering discovered. On the 15th the first British tanks entered Belsen. There they discovered 35,000 unburied corpses, 5,000 more than the number of inmates who were left alive. Many of these were to die over the next few weeks, as they had reached a point of starvation where they could not be saved. Typhus and other diseases were rampant. The scenes made many of the British soldiers viewing them physically sick.

Reactions to these terrible sights differed from place to place. When American troops liberated Dachau on the 28th the piles of emaciated corpses enraged the soldiers so much that they executed all the guards they could find on the spot. On liberation 33,000 people were left alive inside the camp, of which 2,539 were Jews, and 2,466 of these died of disease and starvation in the days after their liberation.

A less violent response to these atrocities took place at Gardelegen, when on the 13th the advancing Americans came across a barn piled high with the bodies of murdered slave labourers. A German column had apparently grown

*Men of the US 42nd Infantry Division in front of the Munich Burger Bräu Keller, cradle of the Nazi movement, following the capture of the Bavarian capital on the 29th. Here in 1923 Adolf Hitler launched his first bid for power with the so-called 'Munich Putsch'. After he came to power the site became a shrine to the Nazi faithful.*

tired of escorting their prisoners and had crushed over 1,000 of them into a locked barn and set it alight. Any prisoners managing to tunnel their way under the barn's foundations were shot in the head as they emerged. The German troops had received help in these horrendous deeds from members of the local police force, and even some of the town's population. In response, the Americans made all the male residents of the town turn out to retrieve the bodies and give them individual decent Christian burials nearby.

There were literally hundreds of documented atrocities uncovered by the advancing Allies during this period, from camps where hundreds of thousands of people were put to death, to incidents where individuals were callously executed at the roadside. At least by the end of the month there was little in the way of the Reich left to continue with these evil and barbaric practices.

**opposite** *British soldiers fight their way through Arnhem for the second time on the 14th. The Dutch town, which had seen heavy fighting in September 1944 during 'Operation Market-Garden' was at last liberated on the 15th. The town suffered yet more damage as the British had to drive the Germans back street by street.*
**below** *A Churchill Crocodile flame-throwing tank assaults an enemy position near the Senio river, Italy, on the afternoon of the 9th. These tanks were used to destroy German bunkers that would otherwise have held up the advance of the 2nd New Zealand Division in this sector.*

**above** *As the British offensive into Holland continued, troops liberated areas from which the V2 rocket had been launched at Britain. A whole train load of rockets was captured along with much associated technical equipment. Here a V2 leaves its launch pad. This one is not destined to kill any innocent civilians. It is a captured rocket being tested by the British authorities.*

**above** US Fifth Army infantrymen fire at German snipers in the centre of Modena on the 22nd. A group of Italian civilians shelter behind the armoured protection of the M3 half-track.

**left** Dr Klein, the SS doctor at Belsen concentration camp admits helping to kill thousands of former inmates to a Movietone news team. He stands in front of a mass grave of as yet unburied victims. Dr Klein admitted that some of those murdered had been subjected to cruel medical experiments, such as the injection of benzine into their bloodstreams. Here, on the 21st, a woman survivor confronts Dr Klein.

**opposite** On the 13th, men of the Third US Army liberated the concentration camp at Buchenwald. What they found horrified them. Only 7,000 inmates survived of a camp that had once held 70,000. The people who lived, Jews and political prisoners, were human skeletons, many unable to walk or eat. Disease was rife throughout the camp. This photograph shows the interior of one of the huts in which the prisoners slept. Two camp doctors, when interrogated, stated that 6,000 prisoners had been killed in March alone. In the winter of 1939 there had been 900 deaths a day.

**above** *British soldiers and German workmen give first aid to a group of Russian women slave workers who had become overcome by smoke and fumes in the cellar of a shop in Osnabrück on the 9th. The women, starving and with little in the way of clothing, had broken into the shop to loot items left behind by its owner, who had fled. A German policeman had seen the break-in and had waited for all the women to enter before setting the building ablaze. Two women were killed in the fire. This photograph shows that the Nazi sentiment of treating Slavs as non-humans still held sway in some German minds even at this late stage in the war.*

**above** *Adolf Hitler awards the Iron Cross, second class to Alfred Czech, a twelve-year-old Hitler Youth soldier who fought in the battles in Pomerania and Upper Silesia in mid-April 1945. Shortly after this picture was taken Berlin was attacked by the Soviets. A few days later Hitler committed suicide.*

**below** *WRNS plotters monitor cross-Channel shipping movements at Naval HQ, Chatham, on the 16th.*

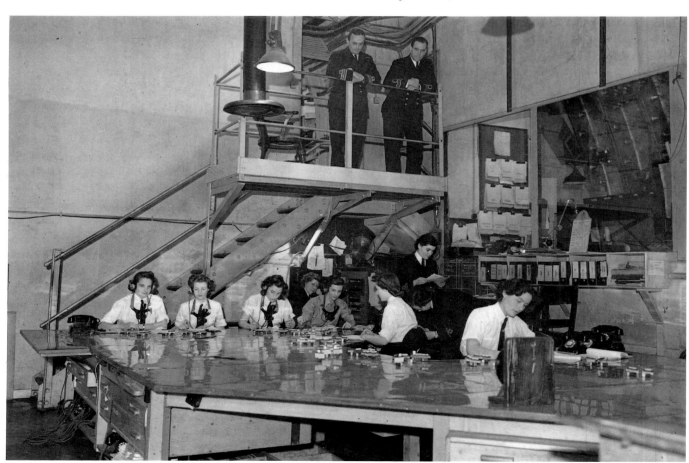

**left** When troops of the US Ninth Army discovered the bodies of over 1,000 slave workers who had been burnt alive in a barn by retreating German soldiers, they made an equal number of male residents of the nearby town of Gardelegen turn out to give each one a decent burial. The townsfolk were formed up in the square and marched off to take the bodies from the barn to a site where they could be given a Christian burial.

**overleaf** US Sherman tanks rumble down the Dachauerstrasse in Munich.

**below** Captain Fedor Lipatkin, Hero of the Soviet Union and commander of a Soviet Guards tank unit, hoists the Red Banner above a captured block of houses in Berlin. Captain Lipatkin was one of the few men of his unit to fight to the German capital all the way from Stalingrad.

# MAY 1945

## *Victory in Europe*

WESTERN FRONT. The month opened with Hamburg Radio announcing to the German people that Hitler had been killed 'fighting for Germany' and that Grand Admiral Karl Doentiz headed the new Flensburg Government. It was clear that the days of the Third Reich were numbered. During the remaining week of the war in Europe, German forces tried to hold the line against the advancing Soviets while arranging for their capitulation to the advancing Western Allies coming up behind them.

May 1. In the British Second Army sector, units of the 8th Corps advanced towards Lübeck and Hamburg. The US Ninth Army ended its last offensive with the 13th, 19th and 16th Corps dug in along the Elbe. The US Seventh Army continued with the mopping up of the Munich area.

2. The US 13th Corps made contact with the Red Army. Meanwhile the 5th Corps of the US First Army pushed on across the Czechoslovak frontier. Negotiations for the surrender of Innsbruck opened between the US 6th Corps and its German defenders. The French 1st Corps reached Obersdorf and Goetzis deep inside Austria.

3. The British 12th Corps received the surrender of the Hamburg garrison. The British 8th Corps pushed on rapidly towards the Kiel Canal. German representatives visited Field Marshal Montgomery's HQ to negotiate a surrender. They were told by the British commander that any capitulation in Northern Europe would have to include surrender to the Soviets as well as the Western Allies.

4. After considering Montgomery's demands the officers returned. The unconditional surrender of all German forces in Holland, Northern Germany and Denmark took place at 6.20 p.m. at Montgomery's HQ on Lüneberg Heath.

On the same day Salzburg surrendered to the US 15th Corps, whose units immediately pushed on towards Berchtesgaden, Hitler's alpine retreat. The US 6th Corps accepted the surrender of Innsbruck. All along the front line with the US Armies, German commanders sought out their opposite numbers to negotiate the surrender of their units.

6. Fighting in the west had by now almost everywhere come to an end. The 97th Division of the US 5th Corps liberated Pilsen in Czechoslovakia. The US 12th Corps advanced rapidly towards Prague hoping to get there before Soviet units arrived.

7. At 1.41 a.m., in Eisenhower's HQ at Rheims, General-oberst Alfred Jodl signed the unconditional surrender of all German Armed Forces to the Allies. The surrender was

**opposite** *A lorry overflowing with revellers races down the Strand in London celebrating VE Day.*

*A British infantryman shakes hands with his Soviet counterpart after the troops had met near Wismar on the 3rd. A crowd of Russian soldiers pose for the cameraman around and on top of a Red Army assault gun.*

effective from midnight on the 9th. However, all military activity against the Western Allies had already ceased.

EASTERN FRONT. The last days of the war on this front had seen the end of the struggle for Berlin and the surrender of the last remaining fortress cities. In the German capital, Soviet forces continued to mop up the last centres of German resistance.

2. Berlin was declared under total Russian control. German leaders, such as Martin Bormann, one of Hitler's closest advisers, fled the capital. Others, such as Goebbels, committed suicide, the Reich propagandist also having his wife and six children killed. The garrison commander, General Krebs, also took his own life.

3. Soviet units of the 2nd Belorussian Front linked up with British forces near Wismar on the 3rd. The Allies had now linked up from the Baltic in the north to Austria in the south.

5. The heaviest fighting was on the Czechoslovakian and Balkan Fronts. In Prague, a full-scale civil uprising began, Czech patriots hoping to liberate their capital before Soviet units arrived. The 150,000 men of German Army Group E were trapped against the Adriatic when Yugoslav forces linked with New Zealand troops in Trieste.

6. The surrounded German forces in Breslau were forced to surrender.

8. VE (Victory in Europe) Day. The last major German cities, Dresden and Görlitz, surrendered to armies of the 1st Ukranian Front. The German surrender to the Russians was signed at Karlshorst, near Berlin, although fighting continued spasmodically for the next two or three days on sectors of the Eastern Front. The war in Europe was now effectively at an end.

The end of the war brought sadness as well as joy to many people. Here a WAAF says a tearful farewell to her American Air Force Sergeant sweetheart as he prepares to board his plane back to the States.

A happy elderly woman sings along with the crowd enjoying VE Day in Piccadilly circus.

A young woman, happy that the war is over, holds up a newspaper proclaiming the Allied victory in Europe.

Local residents dance around a bonfire somewhere in East Acton on VE night.

A crowd gathers outside Buckingham Palace in readiness for the King and
Queen to make an appearance on the royal balcony.

Princess Elizabeth, Queen Elizabeth, Sir Winston Churchill, King George VI
and Princess Margaret wave to the crowds from the balcony of
Buckingham Palace on VE Day.

**MAY 1945**

**above** *Children enjoy a VE Day street party in Brockley, south London.*

**opposite above** *Crowds dance in the street near Berkeley Square, London, on hearing the news of the German surrender.*

**opposite below** *VE Day celebrations in Piccadilly Circus.*

**left** *A woman is hoisted to a vantage point where she can see the crowds, VE Day, Piccadilly Circus.*

**left** *Two smiling girls dressed in Union Jack and Stars and Stripes flags prepare to join the VE celebrations in the centre of Brussels.*

**opposite above left** *A crowd of youngsters, fans of Tito's communist partisans, celebrate VE Day in Trieste.*

**opposite above right** *Pretty Danish girls bring bouquets of flowers to greet RAF airmen as they land in Copenhagen on the 7th.*

**right** *Crowds gather on the Champs-Elysées, Paris, to celebrate VE Day.*

**left** *The citizens of Oslo had to wait several days longer to celebrate their liberation. Here a group of Norwegian children watch the march past of British troops through the city on the 11th.*

## MAY 1945

**left** *The people of Paris, including two soldiers on top of a lamppost, celebrate VE Day in front of the Opera House.*

**opposite** *The surrender document ending the war in North Germany and the Low Countries, signed at Lüneberg Heath on the 4th.*

**left** *The mastheads of Britian's national dailies announce the end of the war in Europe.*

Instrument of Surrender

of

All German armed forces in HOLLAND, in

northwest Germany including all islands,

and in DENMARK.

1. The German Command agrees to the surrender of all German armed
forces in HOLLAND, in northwest GERMANY including the FRISIAN
ISLANDS and HELIGOLAND and all other islands, in SCHLESWIG-
HOLSTEIN, and in DENMARK, to the C.-in-C. 21 Army Group.
*This to include all naval ships in these areas.*
These forces to lay down their arms and to surrender unconditionally.

2. All hostilities on land, on sea, or in the air by German forces
in the above areas to cease at 0800 hrs. British Double Summer Time
on Saturday 5 May 1945.

3. The German command to carry out at once, and without argument or
comment, all further orders that will be issued by the Allied
Powers on any subject.

4. Disobedience of orders, or failure to comply with them, will be
regarded as a breach of these surrender terms and will be dealt
with by the Allied Powers in accordance with the accepted laws
and usages of war.

5. This instrument of surrender is independent of, without prejudice
to, and will be superseded by any general instrument of surrender
imposed by or on behalf of the Allied Powers and applicable to Germany
and the German armed forces as a whole.

6. This instrument of surrender is written in English and in German.

The English version is the authentic text.

7. The decision of the Allied Powers will be final if any doubt or
dispute arises as to the meaning or interpretation of the surrender
terms.

*B. L. Montgomery*
*Field-Marshal*

*4 BLM May 1945*
*1830 hrs*

**above** British soldiers raise a rousing cheer as they hear news of the end of the war via Churchill's radio broadcast.

**below** French female political prisoners and male prisoners of war, happy to be free, walk towards their country's frontier on VE Day.

Men of the 5th Battalion Seaforth Highlanders clear houses of the enemy in Bremervorde in one of the last actions of the war on the 2nd.

Tanks of the US Seventh Army roll through the streets of Garmisch-Partenkirchen, the Bavarian winter sports capital, on the 2nd. It was here that the Germans held the Winter Olympics of 1936.

**below** Captain J. McMahon carries a small child over the river Elbe at Tangemunde. The infant's mother, a slave labourer, had earlier collapsed on their trek back to France.

**below** Two German soldiers, carrying their children, walk into the Allied line to surrender on the 3rd. Their wives follow a few steps behind. Towards the end of the war many soldiers and their families fled west to escape the vengeance of the conquering Red Army.

# MAY 1945

The three ceremonies that saw the end of the war in Europe. First, General Mark Clark, Commander Allied Forces, Italy (left), accepts the surrender of the German forces in Italy. Second, Field Marshal Montgomery reads out the terms of surrender at Lüneberg Heath, northern Germany on the 4th. Third, Generaloberst Alfred Jodl signs the instrument of surrender that offically brought the Second World War in Europe to an end in Rheims on the 8th.

Grand Admiral Doenitz (centre) leaves the German High Command HQ under arrest on the 11th. The last Führer, Doenitz had become Dictator of Germany on the death of Hitler.

**below left** New York crowds celebrate the surrender of Germany in a traditional manner with a parade and clouds of tickertape and confetti.

**below right** Even the citizens of neutral countries celebrated the end to the war which had caused so much suffering the world over. Here the inhabitants of Stockholm march through the streets of the Swedish capital.

# Index